THE TIMES

GOING UNDE[RGROUND]

KW-554-275

PARIS BY METRO

Mike Gerrard

navigator guides

Published by Navigator Guides
www.navigatorguides.com

Published by Navigator Guides
The Old Post Office, Swanton Novers,
Melton Constable, Norfolk NR24 2AJ
www.navigatorguides.com
info@navigatorguides.com

ISBN 1 903872 11 1
ISBN 13: 978-1 903872 11 1
A catalogue record for this book is available from the British Library.

Colour reproduction PDQ Digital
Printed in Italy by Printer Trento srl

Publisher: Rupert Wheeler
Managing editor: Antonia Cunningham
Editor: Susannah Wight
Cover design: Horacio Monteverde
Cover Photo: © Horacio Monteverde
Inside front Métro map © Communicarta Ltd
Inside back map © PC Graphics (UK) Ltd
Typeset in The Sans and Mittleschrift

CONTENTS

INTRODUCTION

We take the Paris Métro so much for granted that it's easy to forget just what an important part of the city's history it is. The Métro is as much an aspect of Paris life as its museums, parks, streets and markets. The first line opened in 1900 and within a few years there was a comprehensive network of lines and stations that transformed the life of the city. People could get around town much more easily – whether going to the big market at Les Halles, visiting the theatre, or getting from one mainline station to another. Life was suddenly better.

Although the groundwork was done in those early days, the Métro is now even more extensive. Made up of some 210km (131 miles) of track, with only 16.6km (10 miles) in the open air, the network is far from finished. There are 14 lines and plans to extend several of them even further into the Paris suburbs.

For the purposes of this book, lines 3, 5, 13 and 14 have been omitted as all the city centre attractions can be easily reached using the other lines.

HOW TO USE THIS BOOK

This book is as easy to navigate as Paris is by Métro. Each section is devoted to one line: Lines 1, 2, 4, 6, 7, 8, 9, 10, 11, 12. Taken together, these lines service every major Métro stop in central Paris that has something of interest close by. There is also a chapter called Further Afield, if you have more time and wish to visit places, such as Versailles or Resort Disneyland® Paris that are outside central Paris on the Métro or its RER (local rail) connections..

Organization

- Under each stop, the sights above ground are listed in order of walking time from the Métro station.

Abbesses Métro station

- Where appropriate, sights have been organized into a straightforward route.
- Where attractions are in a different direction, one direction is followed first before returning to the station and following the sights in the next direction.
- You will be aware that this has happened when an attraction has a shorter walking time than the entry that precedes it.
- The first two pages of each section act as a contents list for the Métro line in question and show you the order of stations (either going north to south or east to west) as well as the places you can visit at each station.
- If a station is an intersection between lines, attractions may be described in a section for another line and there will be a page reference for you to find the entry. These are marked, *see* p.00.
- Stations that are intersection stations and service more than one line are indicated with coloured squares that relate to the colours of each line on the Métro map. For example Opéra is on lines 8, 7 and 3, and will be shown on all the openers of all these lines with two coloured squares next to it to indicate the other lines. So on Line 8 it will have a pale pink ■ and an olive green ■ square next to it, and so on.

- The opener line contents start with the first Métro station on the line that has a listing and continue to the last one that has a listing, including all the stations in between, whether they have a listing or not. This means that you can use this to count off the stations as you go through them.
- Only the stations that have a listing are shown in the rest of the section.

The line or route you take is a matter of choice or convenience. If you have an attraction in mind, consult the index on p.185 and it will direct you to the entry and the station that you need. Then look at the Métro map on the inside front cover of this book to see the best way to get there. Alternatively, you may want to explore a single line. On Line 1, for example, you could spend the morning visiting the Arc de Triomphe; the avenue George V, with its smart shops and American cathedral; move on towards the famous Champs-Elysées; stop for a coffee to watch the world go by and perhaps have a spot of lunch; then spend the afternoon at the Louvre, taking in lovely place Vendôme and the rue de Rivoli along the way. Alternatively, visit any or all of the Musée Carnavalet, Musée Cognacq-Jay and the Musée National Picasso and have lunch or supper in the atmospheric Marais, finishing off perhaps with a trip to the Opéra at the Bastille. **Note that for the purposes of this book, lines and stations have been chosen for each sight, but other lines and stations may also be appropriate**.

Maps and Interchanges

You will need to use this book in conjunction with a good street map (Michelin's *Paris par arrondissements* is a good one in a kind of A-Z format), not only to check the location of the attractions but also to see where the Métro stations are. Generally, stations on the same line in the central area are an average of only about 0.5km (0.3 miles) apart, but this increases the further out you travel. Like other underground maps, the map of the Métro is not to scale so you may find it easier to walk from one line to another one rather than take the train. Then again, sometimes it's quicker to take the train as stations that appear close together on the Métro map may not be quite so close together on the street map

You should also be aware that some interchanges between lines can involve a long walk, even when they share the same station. At some major hubs you can find yourself walking for several minutes to get from one line to another, so if you're only going one stop it may be quicker to leave the station.

Restaurants and Cafés

Recommendations for lunchtime cafés and restaurants are listed for many of the stations and you will never be more than a short walk or two Métro stops away from a recommendation.

Inexpensive	Under €20
Moderate	€20-35
Expensive	over €35

Opening times

All opening times are given in the text Note that most places are shut on 24/25th December and 1st January, as well as other public holidays. Please call or check the website for opening hours at these times.

MÉTRO INFORMATION

The Métro is so reliable and inexpensive that many visitors don't even consider using any other transport and join the four million people who use the system every day. One ticket will take you anywhere in the network, and. you seldom wait more than a few minutes on any line in the central area although, naturally, trains are less frequent the further out you travel and outside peak times of day.

How to Get Round the Métro

The Paris Métro is very easy and logical to use. When finding your train, you need to look for both the line number and the name of the end station, which tells you the direction of travel. So, if you're at the Arc de Triomphe and want to go to the Louvre, you follow the signs for Line 1 Château de Vincennes, as that is the direction of travel. If you follow signs for Line 1 La Défense, you'll find yourself heading in the opposite direction. Forget about the points of the compass and the colour codes on the map for the different lines. Just find the line number and the name of the end station you want to head towards. The RER lines are indicated by letters not numbers. There are complete maps in the ticket offices and on each platform, while each carriage also has a map of that particular line, so you have to be very careless to get lost.

If you're making a change look along the platform and find the orange signs that say CORRESPONDANCE. This tells you where the exit is to connect to another line, and again you will need to know the number of the line and the direction of travel. The signs marked SORTIE are the exits to the streets, and if you check a good street map beforehand you should be able to work out which is the best for your destination.

The Time to Travel

The Métro runs seven days a week from about 5.30am to 12.30am, depending on the line and station. Check first and last train times at individual stations. The RER trains run from about 5am until 12.30am.

Métro Tickets

One ticket is valid for any length of journey within the Métro system, and for buses and RER trains within zones 1 and 2 in the city centre. If you travel beyond zones 1 and 2 on the RER (but not the Métro), you will need to buy the appropriate ticket before travelling. You can switch from Métro to

RER on the same ticket for the same journey, but you can't change from Métro or RER to bus, or from bus to bus, on the same ticket.

Your Métro ticket is valid until you leave the system. You must stamp it in the machine when you enter, which normally also opens the gates to let you in, and keep it with you till you go out through the exit gates in case an inspector asks to see it. Once you're through the exit gates, throw the ticket away as it has now been time-stamped and cannot be used again.

Tickets can be bought at the station, at tourist information offices and at some tobacconists. If you're going to be using the Métro a few times during your visit, it is cheaper to buy 10 tickets: ask for a carnet ('kar-nay'). Children under 4 travel free of charge, and under 11 pay approximately half the adult fare.

Single Fare

Zone 1	€1.40
Carnet of 10 tickets	€10.50

1-day Mobilis Pass

Valid on the day of purchase for all Métro, RER and bus journeys within the zones paid for but excludes airports.

Zones 1 and 2	€5.80
Zones 1–9	€18.30

Paris Visite pass

Issued for 1, 2, 3 or 5 days, and within zones 1–3 or 1–5. Zone 5 will take you as far as Versailles and Resort Paris Disneyland® (*see* pp.177 and 179) and the airports. They are valid from the first time you use them, and for all Métro, RER and bus journeys within the given zones. They also include discounts on admission to some attractions but although they simplify things they are usually the most expensive option.

Zones 1–3	1 day	€8.35
	2 days	€13.70
	3 days	€18.25
	5 days	€26.65

Zones 1–5	1 day	€16.75
	2 days	€26.65
	3 days	€37.35
	5 days	€45.70
Zones 1–8	1 day	€23.60
	2 days	€34.30
	3 days	€42.65
	4 days	€53.35

Carte Orange Pass
This provides unlimited travel for either a week or a month in any zone you want, but you will need to provide a passport photograph when applying for one. Both cover all Métro and bus travel and also zones 1–2 on the RER trains.

Coupon Hebdomadaire
This runs from Monday to Sunday. They are aimed at commuters and are only good value if you arrive early in the week.

Zones 1–2 €14.50

Coupon Mensuel
This is valid until the end of the month in which you buy it – don't buy one on the 30th of the month.

Zones 1–2 €48.60.

Métro Etiquette

For the comfort and safety of everyone using the Métro, there are a few easy rules that you should follow:

- When on escalators, stand on the right so that people who want to walk up can pass you on the left.
- When you get on the train, move away from the doors so that there is space for other people to get on.
- If you are using one of the flip-up seats near the doors and the carriage starts to get crowded, you are expected to stand to create more space.
- Plan your route so you can move through the station easily. Do not stop at the bottom of stairs if there are people behind you.
- Keep all your luggage with you at all times.
- Avoid travelling with luggage at peak times.

- Do not eat smelly food on the Métro.
- It is forbidden to smoke anywhere on the Métro or in the Métro station.
- As a safety precaution, there are no litter bins in the Métro network so please take your litter with you.
- Be alert for any unattended bags. If you see something that looks suspicious, contact the nearest staff member.

Métro Safety

Thieves

Stations and trains are generally clean and safe although, as in most major cities, you need to be careful about pickpockets and other petty thieves, so take the usual precautions, keeping your money hidden and your bags properly closed. Women should keep the front of their handbags inward so that fastenings are not accessible to other people. If you have a shoulder bag, think about putting the strap over your head, so that it cannot be removed easily by somebody else. You also need to be wary when the doors are about to close – a favourite time for someone to snatch a bag and run. Also, take extra care when using the escalators, especially if someone is close behind you.

Scams

A recent scam is to offer to help people buy their Métro tickets from a machine, especially the new arrivals on Eurostar at Gare du Nord station. Beware the seemingly kindly gentleman taking pity on your confusion. He will either hand you a stack of 10 dud tickets, the uselessness of which you won't be aware of until you try to use the first one, or will simply take your money and run. By and large the Métro is perfectly safe, but you should take the precautions you would take in any big city.

Beggars and buskers

As in many cities, on the trains you will find beggars and buskers. Neither are encouraged, and most passengers ignore them.

Arc de Triomphe

LINE 1
LA DÉFENSE – CHÂTEAU DE VINCENNES

The first Métro line in Paris, Line 1, opened on 19 July 1900 and ran east–west across the city, from Porte de Vincennes to Porte Maillot. In 1932 the eastern end was extended as far as the current terminus, Château de Vincennes. In 1937 two more stations were added in the west, and in 1992 the western end of the line was extended out to La Défense.

Line 1 is useful for tourists as it goes through some of the city's main attractions, such as the Arc de Triomphe, the Louvre, the Tuileries Gardens, the place de la Concorde and the Marais district and, further west, past the place de la Bastille all the way to the Bois de Vincennes. This, then, is the line of royal palaces and gardens, famous squares like Bastille and Concorde, and ancient mansions of the Marais out to the modern commercial mansions that are the futuristic office-blocks of La Défense.

Arc de Triomphe

CHARLES DE GAULLE ÉTOILE

Arc de Triomphe (0 mins)

***Tel**: (01) 55 37 73 77*
***Open**: Apr–Sep daily 10am–11pm*
***Adm**: adult €7, 18–25s €4.50, under-18s free*

The Arc de Triomphe, one of Paris's great landmarks, was begun in 1806, to celebrate Napoleon's victory at the Battle of Austerlitz in 1805, but it wasn't completed until 1836, which was partly due to Napoleon's subsequent fall from power and popularity. In 1840, his funeral procession passed beneath it and today it is a focal point for demonstrations and meetings, for funeral processions and sporting events. The Tomb of the Unknown Soldier, symbolizing the sacrifice of all those killed during World War I is also here; the torch on the tomb is symbolically re-ignited each day at 6.30pm.

The Arc stands in the middle of one of the busiest traffic junctions in the city. 'Etoile' means 'star', and this spot has 12 roads radiating from it; its impressive design can be best appreciated by climbing the 284 steps or taking the elevator to the top and enjoying the view from 50m (164ft) above the traffic.

From the top you can also see that the Arc de Triomphe is on a straight axis between the modern Grande Arche at La Défense and the Arche du Carrousel and glass pyramid at the Louvre. A small but enjoyable museum tells the history of the Arc, and it is worth getting up close to appreciate the elaborate carvings that adorn every side. The 30 shields that run around the top of the arch each celebrate a different Napoleonic victory.

Dragons Élysées

11 rue de Berri

Tel: (01) 42 89 85 10

Open: Daily, lunch and dinner

Moderate

Eat Chinese food in Paris? Well, yes, when it's as good as it is here. The Dragons provides Thai dishes, too, and children will be impressed with its huge underfloor aquarium.

GEORGE V

The Lido (1 min)

116bis avenue des Champs-Élysées

***Tel**: (01) 40 76 56 10; www.lido.fr*

***Open**: daily from 7.30pm dinner, 9.30pm show, extra show Sat midnight*

***Adm**: adults €70–160, under-12s €25*

Paris has long been the home of cabaret and shows, usually featuring scantily clad dancers, and the Lido, on the left as you walk down the Champs-Elysées from the Arc de Triomphe, is one of the most famous. There have been shows here since the 1920s (the name came from the Lido beach in Venice), but it was only after World War II that the modern Lido came into being. It is renowned as the home of the Bluebell Girls, the troupe of tall, long-legged dancers, many of whom over the years have, in fact, been English rather than French. Today the troupe is 60-strong, an impressive sight.

Although the shows have become a regular part of the tourist trail, kept in business by coachloads of overseas visitors turning up every evening, they are still spectacular shows into which a lot of money, effort and creativity is poured. Special effects such as aerial ballets and skating rinks built into the stage combine

with a hearty dinner, for which here at Le Lido one of the country's top chefs, Lyon-based Paul Bocuse, designed the menus. The theatre is 6000 square metres in size and holds 1150 seats, so while the shows are not cheap, an impressive night out is definitely assured.

Avenue George V (1 min)

Avenue George V is yet another of Paris's grand streets, heading due south from the Champs-Élysées at the junction where you find **Fouquet's** restaurant. This itself is a Paris tradition, dating back to 1899 and boasting the Irish writer James Joyce as one of its regular customers when he lived in the city. It is expensive, like everything on the Champs-Élysées, but dining there or having a coffee looking out onto the street is a very Parisian experience.

A short way down on the right is the **Bar Fly**, a fashionable hang-out where the glitzy and famous congregate, and where you won't get in without the doorman's approval. Further down is one of the city's finest hotels, the **George V**, whose famous guests have included Duke Ellington, the Beatles and the Rolling Stones. It was recently revamped and now boasts a Michelin-starred restaurant. If you can't afford to stay here, at least look into the

Fouquet's

99 avenue des Champs-Élysées

Tel: (01) 47 23 70 60

Open: Daily, 8am–2am

Expensive

Revered old standby right on the Champs-Élysées where you'll pay highly for a cup of coffee on the terrace, but it does have a very good reputation for food if you want a splurge.

La Grande Armée

3 avenue de la Grande-Armée

Tel: (01) 45 00 24 77

Open: Daily, 7am–2am

Moderate

There's a slight Napoleonic theme to this excellent brasserie near the Arc de Triomphe, the perfect place to call in for a light lunch, a snack or a drink with everything from burgers to fancier foods.

Courtyard of the American Cathedral on Avenue Georges V

Restaurant Cap Vernet

82 avenue Marceau

Tel: (01) 47 20 20 40; www.guysavoy.com

Open: Mon–Fri lunch and dinner, Sat dinner

Expensive

Smart fish restaurant run by top chef Guy Savoy, though it's possible to eat there at lunchtime without breaking the bank. Oysters are a speciality.

Spoon, Food and Wine

14 rue de Marignan

Tel: (01) 40 76 34 44; www.spoon.tm.fr

Open: Mon–Fri lunch and dinner

Moderate

Spoon was the Michelin-starred chef Alain Ducasse's first venture into more affordable cuisine, although it is still not cheap. The fun is in choosing not only your main dish but the sauce it comes with and the accompanying side dish, too, but you could also have the chef's choice or the Speedy Spoon menu if you're in a hurry.

reception area or pop into the bar to enjoy a brief look at the opulence and the stunning displays of flowers.

Keep walking down further towards the Seine and you reach the late 19th-century Gothic **American Cathedral**, which was consecrated at the same time as the French-built Statue of Liberty was put up in New York. In total contrast, further down on the other side of the road at number 12 is another famous Paris cabaret, the **Crazy Horse Saloon**, which goes back to the 1950s.

FRANKLIN D. ROOSEVELT

Franklin D. Roosevelt Métro station (0 mins)

Guidebooks are fond of trotting out the fact that this is the oldest Métro station in Paris, and it's certainly a distinctive station for its décor, as long as you don't expect a slice of ancient history. Many stations were built at the same time – otherwise there wouldn't have been a Métro line – and this was merely one of the first. It was originally called Marbeuf-Rond Point des Champs-Elysées, and was renamed in honour of the US President after the war in 1946. Soon after this work started on a station modernization programme, when each station was given its own visual style, rather than have them all conforming to the same model, as had been the case in the past. Franklin D. Roosevelt was the first of these, in 1952, and it is from this date that the station's now rather dour but distinctive look originates.

Avenue Montaigne (1 min)

In the 19th century this elegant street was the focus of Paris nightlife, but today the focus is very much on fashion. All the designer names are here on this short stretch, so, whether you want to buy or just browse, head southwest from the Métro station towards the river and be prepared to see some of the most famous names in the world. Christian Dior (no.30), MaxMara (no.31), Valentino (17–19), Chanel (no.42) Calvin Klein (no.53) are all here. Other names include Prada, Jil Sander, Nina Ricci, Emanuel Ungaro and Vivienne Westwood.

It's not all about fashion, though. As you make your way towards the river you'll pass some swish hotels and smart restaurants, including the Plaza-Athénée hotel where Alain Ducasse, arguably the country's top chef, serves some of the finest food on the planet. A meal here can cost the earth but is worth it even if you only ever have one once in your life. The street also boasts two theatres: the Comédie des Champs-Élysées and the Théâtre des Champs-Élysées.

Avenue Montaigne

Avenue Matignon (1 min)

In the opposite direction from the avenue Montaigne is the avenue Matignon. Here the shopping shifts from designer fashion to arts and antiques, although it doesn't necessarily get any cheaper. This avenue is particularly known for galleries that sell the best of contemporary fine art, such as Maurice Garnier and Daniel Malingue. There is also a specialist stamp collectors' market here and on the adjacent avenue Gabriel on Thursdays, Saturdays and Sundays. If you follow the street it leads to the equally fashionable Faubourg St-Honoré, with more designer names.

Bar des Théâtres

6 avenue Montaigne

Tel: (01) 47 23 34 63

Open: Daily, 6am–2am, food all day

Inexpensive

A real mix of people frequent this very down-to-earth café–bar, including those who work in the avenue's stylish fashion stores, actors attending rehearsals at the theatre and audiences before and after the night's show. The food is simple, and available almost 24 hours a day.

Palais de la Découverte (5 mins)

Avenue Franklin D. Roosevelt

***Tel**: (01) 56 43 20 21; www.palais-decouverte.fr*

***Open**: Tue–Sat 9.30am–6pm, Sun 10am–7pm*

***Adm**: adults €5.60, 5–18 and concessions €3.70, under-5s free; planetarium €3.10*

Housed in one wing of the Grand Palais, this science museum is fun for both adults and children. There are lots of interactive displays, which children love, and the museum tries to strike a balance between making the exhibits both informative and fun. They range from metal models of dinosaurs through models and designs of some of Leonardo da Vinci's inventions to contemporary science with the chance to see what a nuclear reaction is like.

Other displays include holographs and astronomy, with one room devoted to the sun, while at weekends and during school holidays there are usually special talks and displays aimed at educating children. For these and other shows at the planetarium, ring ahead or check the website for details of the current programme.

CHAMPS-ÉLYSÉES CLÉMENCEAU

Champs-Élysées (0 mins)

This must be the most famous street name in Paris although, with its fast-food restaurants, record stores and car showrooms, these days it's a long way from the Elysian Fields that gave it its name. Strolling along here is still an essential part of the Paris experience, though, especially if you walk up the street towards the Arc de Triomphe at the crown of the small hill. It's one of the most magnificent sights in the city and on a sunny day a coffee in one of the sidewalk cafés completes the feel – though check the price first!

Le Champs-Elysées

Galeries Nationales du Grand Palais

Galeries Nationales du Grand Palais (2 mins)

3 avenue du Général-Eisenhower
***Tel**: (01) 44 13 17 17; www.rmn.fr*
***Open**: Thu–Mon 10am–8pm, Wed 10am–10pm*
***Adm**: adults €10.10 until 1pm with a reservation (recommended), €9 after 1pm, concessions and 18–26s €8 (before 1pm), €5.50 (after 1pm), under 13s free*

The Grand Palais was built in 1900 for the Paris Exposition, which also introduced the Petit Palais and the Eiffel Tower to the city. The magnificent belle époque architecture is crowned by an impressive glass roof. There are bronze horses and chariots at each corner of the roof, although at the time of writing these are being restored, along with the rest of the building, which is due to have reopened by early 2006 latest. The palace will continue to house special art and fine art exhibitions, and so call first or check listings magazines to find out what is on. It's often the place where the block-buster art exhibitions that tour the world are shown in Paris, and even if you are not interested in a particular exhibition, it is worth looking inside to see the architecture.

Petit Palais (3 mins)

Avenue Winston-Churchill
***Tel**: (01) 44 51 19 31*
***Open**: closed for renovation until autumn 2005*

The 'Little Palace', built at the same time as the Grand Palais, but as implied by the

Laurent

41 avenue Gabriel

Tel: (01) 42 25 00 39; www.le-laurent.com

Open: Mon–Fri lunch and dinner, Sat dinner

Expensive

Not the kind of place you pop into for a coffee and a sandwich, but one of the city's top restaurants. However, the lunchtime fixed-price menu brings *haute cuisine* within the reach of most visitors.

name, less grand, is home to Paris's fine arts museum, the **Musée des Beaux-Arts de la Ville de Paris**, containing furniture, sculpture and the City of Paris collection of 19th-century paintings, with works by names including Cézanne and Monet. However, it is currently closed for restoration and due to reopen in autumn 2005

Pont Alexander III (5 mins)

Continuing south past the Grand Palais and Petit Palais brings you down to the River Seine and the Pont Alexandre II. Walking across this bridge gives you a splendid view of the Hôtel des Invalides on the Left Bank, which is especially memorable on a sunny day. The bridge was also built for the 1900 Exposition, to allow visitors easy access from the Left Bank to the two newly opened palaces. The foundation stone was laid by Alexandre II of Russia, and the bridge named after him. You need to walk along the riverbank a little, or walk across the adjacent Pont de Invalides, to appreciate fully the ornate Art Nouveau architecture.

Palais de L'Élysée, *see* Miromesnil, p.131

Pont Alexander III

Place de la Concorde

CONCORDE

Place de la Concorde (1 min)

At the bottom end of the Champs-Élysées stands the 20-acre (8-hectare) square of the place de la Concorde, looking northwest up towards the Arc de Triomphe. On the southeast side, though not visible behind their boundary walls, are the Tuileries Gardens and beyond them the Louvre.

Like the Arc de Triomphe (***see*** p.14), the huge amount of modern-day traffic can mask the square's grand features and historical origins. It was built between 1755 and 1775 with a statue of Louis XV in the centre, but during the Revolution it was the home instead to the guillotine, and named the place de la Révolution. Over 1,000 people were executed here, including Queen Marie-Antoinette. By 1795 it had been renamed place de la Concorde.

In 1833 the Egyptian government gave one of the obelisks from the Temple of Luxor as a gift to the French government (something it's impossible to imagine happening today), and the 23-m (75-ft) high construction, covered in hieroglyphics, still stands in the centre of the square.

Maxim's

3 rue Royal

Tel: (01) 42 65 27 94; www.maxims-de-paris.com

Open: Mon–Sat lunch and dinner

Expensive

One of the names that sums up Parisian sophistication, Maxim's is now owned by Pierre Cardin and serves dishes of the truffles and foie gras variety in a glorious Belle Époque interior. Definitely one to save for a special treat.

Paris's largest square was designed by architect Jacques-Ange Gabriel, who was also responsible for the grand buildings on the north side, the **Hôtel de la Marine** and the **Hôtel Crillon**, the latter being one of the city's best hotels, with its restaurant one of Paris's temples of *haute cuisine*.

Angelina

226 rue de Rivoli

Tel: (01) 42 60 82 00

Open: Mon–Fri 9.45am–6.45pm, Sat–Sun 9am–7pm

Moderate

This tea room is a Parisian institution, noted for its rich hot chocolate drink. It serves patisseries and lunch.

Jeu de Paume (1 min)

1 place de la Concorde
***Tel**: (01) 47 03 12 50;*
www.cnpphotographie.com

Based inside a 19th-century real tennis court, which is what gives the building its name, the Jeu de Paume has been one of the best exhibition spaces in the city for many years, housing temporary and often provocative and exciting shows. However, it is about to change its purpose, and may even be open again by the time this book appears. It is about to become the base for the new Centre National de la Photographie (National Photography Centre), which is being renamed the **Centre de l'Image Jeu de Paume**.

It seems it will complement the Maison Européenne de la Photographie in the Marais (***see** p.99*) in some ways, as it will feature movies and video as well as still photography, with changing exhibitions from the leading artists in film, video and photography.

Jeu de Paume

Musée de l'Orangerie (2 mins)

Jardin des Tuileries

In the corner of the Tuileries, overlooking the place de la Concorde (***see** p.22*), the Orangerie museum is best known for its eight huge Monet paintings of waterlilies, which have been impressively displayed in a special basement gallery. It also has the Walter-Guillaume collection covering the years 1870–1930, which includes work by famous names such as Renoir, Modigliani and Picasso. So although the Orangerie is a fairly modest building by the standards of some other galleries, it has always housed an unusual and impressive collection.

The museum closed a few years ago for renovation, and was due to reopen in 2003. However, excavations below the building uncovered part of the Louvre's original walls, some of which can be seen to great effect below ground in the Louvre itself. This discovery meant that renovations were put on hold, and a new reopening date of 2005 was estimated, with some people estimating it will be 2006 at least.

TUILERIES

Jardins des Tuileries (0 mins)

It's hard to imagine when you look at the relaxed life of people in the Tuileries Gardens today, that these were once the scenes of revolutionary violence. The gardens used to belong to the French monarchy, but on 20 June 1792 both they and the palace that stood alongside them were stormed by mobs of French citizens, out to overthrow the ruling royalty. This was achieved on 10 August the same year, when King Louis XVI was finally removed from the throne and his Tuileries Palace was sacked, and ransacked.

The palace and gardens had been built in 1564 for Catherine de Médici. A century later in 1664, these were redesigned into formal gardens and opened to the public. Gardens and palace both survived the Revolution,

Jardins des Tuileries

but the palace was finally burned down during the Paris Commune in 1871.

Today the Tuileries are a very popular spot with Parisians and visitors alike. Office workers come to take a lunchtime break, mothers and nannies push kids in buggies, people sit on the benches reading magazines and newspapers, others sit and watch the world go by. There's an ornamental pond and gracing some of the pathways underneath the lime and chestnut trees are statues by several different artists including Giacommetti and Henry Moore. At the time of the aristocracy there were many more sculptures here, but some were taken for display in the Louvre and replaced by copies. Now there is a gradual but ongoing programme to return the gardens to their 17th-century design.

Place Vendôme (5 mins)

From the Métro, walk along the rue de Rivoli, with the Tuileries Gardens on your right, passing the elegant Hôtel Meurice and turn right along the rue de Castiglione. This leads to another of Paris's historic and stylish squares, the place Vendôme, home to the Ritz hotel and smart shopping with names such as as Giorgio Armani, Cartier and Van Clees residing here.

In 1685 the Sun King, Louis XIV, decided this was the perfect spot for a statue of himself, so he bought and demolished the convent that existed here, and the town house of the Duc de Vendôme, which gives the square its name. The equestrian statue was duly erected in the middle, only to be torn down in August 1792 during the Revolution. At the same time the square was also used to display the heads of some of the victims of Madame Guillotine.

The decoration at the centre of the square has since been subject to various changes. In 1806 a column celebrating yet another of Napoleon's victories was put up, topped by a figure of Napoleon dressed as Julius Caesar. In 1814 this was replaced by a statue of Henri IV. In turn, this was replaced by a *fleur-de-lys* design, which gave way to yet another statue of Napoleon. In 1871 the column was destroyed, only to be replaced a few years later by a replica, which has so far managed to stay there for well over a hundred years – a record!

In one corner of the place is the **Ministry of Justice**, while on the other side is the **Hôtel Ritz**, which also has several claims to historical fame. The Ritz Bar (entrance off the rue Cambon) was 'liberated' by the American author Ernest Hemingway, who claims to have been the first to arrive for a drink after the 1944 liberation of Paris from the occupying Germans, and in 1997 it was here that Diana, Princes of Wales, spent the evening before her fatal accident in at the entrance to the underpass beneath the pont de l'Alma, further along the River Seine.

Place Vendôme

PALAIS ROYAL MUSÉE DU LOUVRE

Comédie Française (1 min)

Place Colette
***Tel**: (01) 44 58 15 15; www.comedie-francaise.fr*
***Open**: Box office open daily 11am–6pm*
***Adm**: €10–30*

Formally founded by Louis XIV in 1680, though its roots go back well before then, the prestigious Comédie Française is the city's oldest theatre and still the only one

Café de la Comédie

153 rue St-Honoré

Open: Tue–Sun 10am–midnight

Inexpensive

You can't get more local and more atmospheric than this little café opposite the Comédie Française theatre. Serves excellent, simple grub.

to have its own repertory group of actors. The present theatre near the Louvre was only built in the late 18th century; it's a small but an atmospheric theatre, still putting on performances of the best classical and contemporary dramas.

The theatre is renowned for once being the home of the great French playwright and actor Molière, who died onstage in 1673 as the curtain came down on one of his own plays, *La Malade Imaginaire* (The Imaginary Illness). If you attend a performance here you can go upstairs and see the armchair into which he collapsed and died.

Palais Royal (1 min)

Place du Palais Royal
www.paris.org/monuments/palais.royal
***Open**: gardens open daily dawn–dusk*
***Adm**: free*

First built in 1632 by Cardinal Richelieu, these buildings became the Royal Palace after his death in December 1642 when Anne of Austria lived here with her son, Louis XIV. It then passed into the hands of the Dukes of Orléans and underwent extensive changes; today the buildings contain various state offices. The grounds are open to the public, and the courtyard contains some striking modern sculptures,

Palais Royal

which could hardly be more different from the classical buildings that surround them. The various arcades in and around the palace complex now house art galleries, shops and restaurants, and above them are apartments whose past residents have included Cocteau and Colette.

Place des Victoires (5 mins)

As with the place Vendôme (***see*** p.25), this stylish square was originally designed, in 1685, to highlight yet another statue of Louis XIV. This was destroyed during the Revolution, but replaced in 1822 by an equestrian statue of the king. The square has undergone some changes, however; like the place des Vosges (***see*** p.44) it fell into disrepair, in this case in the 19th century, but was recently renovated to become the home of some high-class fashion stores including Kenzo and Thierry Mugler, shoe stores such as Atelier Voisin and more commonplace names like Timberland and Island.

Equestrian statue of Louis XIV, Place des Victoires

Arc de Triomphe du Carrousel (1 min)

Place du Carrousel

The Arc de Triomphe du Carrousel, which stands near the Louvre, is less grand than the Arc de Triomphe, but also commemorates Napoleonic battle victories of 1805. It was built between 1805 and 1808, and is in a straight line with the Arc de Triomphe, at the far end of the Champs-Élysées – and in turn with the Grande Arche de la Défense. The name 'carrousel' derives from the fact that in 1662, to celebrate the birth of the Dauphin that year (the King's eldest son and heir to the throne), a special fair, horse races and drama productions were mounted on this site, the Jardin du Carrousel.

Musée des Arts Décoratifs
Musée de la Mode et du Textile
Musée de la Publicité (2 mins)

107 rue de Rivoli
Tel: *(01) 44 55 57 50; www.ucad.fr*
Open: *Tue–Fri 11am–6pm, Sat–Sun 10am–6pm*
Adm: *adults €6, 18–25s €4.50, under-18s free*

Heading west along the rue de Rivoli, on the south side of the street, you come to the row of buildings that houses three museums for which you buy your tickets in the same entrance.

Musée des Arts Décoratifs

This museum contains a fine collection of furniture, sculptures, art works, tableware, glass and other objects, including religious items from churches and monasteries.

At the time of writing, it is being revamped, and only the Medieval and Renaissance sections are open to the public, but more is due to reopen in 2005.

Musée de la Mode et du Textile

You might think what is basically a fashion museum might be of limited interest, unless you have a special fascination for the subject, but like the adjoining Musée de la Publicité (***see** below*), it is surprisingly engrossing. The displays change regularly taken from what is the largest collection of 20th-century fashion in the world, with other items that go back to the 18th century. There are over 20,000 different outfits in the archives and almost all of the famous designer names of the last 100 years have donated items. Stylish and/or outrageous, whatever's your interest, this museum has the lot.

Musée de la Publicité

This specialist museum dedicated to the worlds of publicity and advertising is a fascinating treasure trove of material. The bulk of the displays consists of posters down the ages, grouped under specific themes or periods. They range from the most beautiful art posters, through images that we might now find quite shocking, on to material that was once charming but today only provides a chuckle. Again, the international core collection is so huge that only a tiny fraction can be seen at any one time and the displays change regularly. There are also study areas and monitors showing movie ads and publicity.

LOUVRE RIVOLI

Rue de Rivoli (0 mins)

The rue de Rivoli dates back to the early 18th century and was created by Napoleon to commemorate his victory in 1797 against the Austrians at Rivoli.

It runs in an almost straight line from the northeast corner of the place de la Concorde, past the Tuileries Gardens, by the Louvre and on to the Marais, where it undergoes a name change to become the rue Saint-Antoine before ending up at the Bastille. It is mainly the section between the Louvre (***see*** below) and the place de la Concorde (***see*** p.22), though, which everyone thinks about when they hear the name of the rue de Rivoli. This is the stretch where the **grand arcades** are to be found, looking very impressive from across

Rue de Rivoli

the street, though less so from underneath as many of the shops these days are souvenir shops, not many of which sell anything particularly individual. Only the place name on the T-shirt is different. However, there are exceptions, and it's worth putting up with the crowds to see some of the impressively decorated exteriors, the distinguished old hotels and tea shops such as the Meurice and Angelina, elegant tailors and even the Paris branch of WH Smith, here an excellent source of English-language books and journals.

Musée du Louvre (1 min)

Palais du Louvre, Cour Napoleon
***Tel**: (01) 40 20 50 50 and (01) 40 20 51 51 for recorded information; www.louvre.fr*
***Open**: Thu–Sun 9am–6pm, Mon and Wed 9am–9.45pm*
***Adm**: adults €7.50 until 3pm and €5 after 3pm and on Sun, free first Sun of each month and for under-18s*

The Louvre is one of the biggest and best collections of art and antiquities in the world and is spread around extensive buildings. If time allows, it is best to visit more than once, because one day is not near enough time to see everything of interest. If time is limited then it helps to plan and to pick up a leaflet at the

Musée du Louvre

entrance, which gives you a map of the building and shows where the main attractions are. These include works such as the *Mona Lisa* and the *Venus de Milo*, as well as a vast collection of old masters and stunning Egyptian antiquities.

The origins of the Louvre go back to the 13th century, when King Philippe Auguste, who was then living in a palace on the Île de la Cité, had a defensive fortress built here on the north bank of the river. Over the centuries, the fortress was extended and rebuilt, until, eventually, by the 16th century it had become a royal residence.

In 1682 the court moved out to Versailles and the Louvre was abandoned; a colony of artists set up home at one point and it became a complete bohemian city. After the French Revolution at the end of the 18th century the new rulers of France decided that the vast royal collections should be on public display under one roof, for all to see, and the roof they chose was that of the Louvre. Thus the building has had a interesting history; most recently, in 1989, a glass pyramid covering the main entrance to the museum was erected in the courtyard.

Queues to get in via the Pyramid can be very long. Tips to avoid them include arriving before the doors open; waiting until late afternoon; buying tickets in advance on the internet or at stores, including Virgin and Fnac, and using other entrances accessible through the Carrousel from the rue de Rivoli or from the Palais Royal Métro where the queues are often shorter.

Inside, the biggest queues are usually to be found around the *Mona Lisa*, the portrait by Leonardo da Vinci that seems to have become the one 'must-see' exhibit. If you arrive early, make it your first port of call to avoid the crowds. But just about every famous name in art is represented in the galleries, bar the more modern who are exhibited at the Musée d'Orsay and elsewhere. In the Louvre's collections you will find Vermeer, Giotto, Caravaggio, El Greco, Turner, Rembrandt, Bosch, Géricault, Goya...the names run on and on.

The highlight of the sculpture galleries, or rather its most famous exhibit, is the *Venus de Milo*, which is beautifully displayed so you see it from a distance. There are works too by Michaelangelo and Puget, the awe-inspiring *Winged Victory of Samothrace* and the *Marly Horses*, which once stood near the place de la Concorde until they were replaced by replicas and brought here and displayed in one of the covered courtyards.

There are vast collections from the ancient world, including Egyptian, Roman, Greek, Etruscan and Islamic Art, all of which could detain you for a day by itself. Another absorbing section is on the lower ground floor, where the medieval moats, towers and walls of the original fortress have been excavated and are dramatically displayed with theatrical lighting.

To sustain you on your visit there are several eating options, including a café, a snack bar and a formal restaurant, all near the main entrance; the highly rated Café Marly overlooks the pyramid. Alternatively, your museum ticket is valid all day and allows you to leave and return at any time, so head for the Carrousel (***see*** p.29) where there is a choice of self-service restaurants serving a variety of ethnic foods.

St-Germaine l'Auxerrois

St-Germaine l'Auxerrois (2 mins)

2 place du Louvre
***Tel**: (01) 42 60 13 96*
***Open**: Mon–Sat 8am–8pm, Sun 8.30am–8pm*
***Adm**: free*

Behind the Louvre on its eastern side is the church of St-Germaine l'Auxerrois. This was the royal church when the Louvre became the royal palace, though its own history pre-dates even that. The Lady Chapel goes back to the 13th century, when the court was based on the Île de la Cité, and it has been added to and rebuilt over the years, resulting in rather a mish-mash of styles.

This is the church where, on 24 August 1572, the bell rang to mark the St Bartholomew's Day Massacre, on the eve of the wedding between Protestant Henri de Navarre to Marguerite de Valois, the sister of the Catholic King Charles IX. Despite the religious wars at the time, thousands of Protestants were encouraged to come to Paris to celebrate the union. But the king's mother, Catherine de Medici, encouraged him to take his opportunity and attack the Protestant nobles who had gathered in the Louvre palace to help celebrate the wedding. This he did and they were slaughtered as the church bells rang out. An estimated 3000 Protestants were massacred throughout the city, and many more throughout France when news broke out. The resulting civil war was to rage for over 20 years.

HÔTEL DE VILLE

See Line 11, p.146

Hôtel de Ville p.146, Cloîtres des Billettes p.147, Église Saint Merri p.147

ST-PAUL (LE MARAIS)

Rue des Rosiers (1 min)

Parts of the Marais, centred on the rue des Rosiers, have been the Jewish quarter since the 13th century. However, the street name goes back even further, deriving from the rose bushes that used to grow here inside the old city walls. Here you'll find Jewish delis, bakers, restaurants and bookshops – although the street is more cosmopolitan and also one of the city's main gay quarters. It's an intriguing mix, with dusty old shops side by side with cutting-edge designer stores.

Rue des Rosiers

Musée Carnavalet (5 mins)

23 rue de Sévigné
***Tel**: (01) 44 59 58 58;*
www.paris.france.org/musees
***Open**: Tue–Sun 10am–6pm*
***Adm**: free; charge for special exhibitions*

The Carnavalet Museum is an intriguing if sometimes frustrating collection of historical items, especially paintings, which tell the story of the history of Paris.

It opened as a museum in 1880, although the main building, the Hôtel Carnavalet itself, was built in the 1540s for the President of the Paris Parliament. A new wing was added in 1660, designed by the noted architect Mansart, and it later became the home of the 17th century writer Madame de Sévigné.

It was another famous architect, Baron Haussmann, who had the idea for a museum devoted to the history of Paris when he completely redesigned the city in the late 19th century. By 1989 the collection had grown so much that it expanded into the neighbouring mansion, the Hôtel Le Peletier de St-Fargeau.

At the main entrance on the rue de Sévigné there are museum plans in several languages – take one as the layout can be confusing. One of the best parts of the museum is on the second floor of the 'new' wing and is devoted to the French Revolution.

For many visitors the paintings rather than the objects are the most fascinating part of the collection, allowing you to see Paris change – or sometimes remain the same – over the centuries. Also worth noting are the many elaborately decorated rooms, not to mention the re-creation of the cork-lined study in which Marcel Proust used to seek concentration for his writing.

Musée Cognacq-Jay (5 mins)

Hôtel Donon, 8 rue Elzévir
***Tel**: (01) 40 27 07 21*
***Open**: Tue–Sun 10am–6pm*
***Adm**: free; charge for special exhibitions*

A little less celebrated than the Musée Carnavalet, this smaller museum is housed in an old Marais mansion dating from the 16th century but furnished in 18th-century style. Visiting it is a little like visiting a private home, with some displays along small, dark corridors that then lead into large bright rooms where every wall is covered by something eye-catching.

Pitchi Poï

9 place Marché Ste-Catherine

Tel: (01) 42 77 46 15 www.pitchipoi.com

Open: Mon–Sat lunch and dinner, Sun noon–4pm

Moderate

Excellent Jewish restaurant on a lovely hidden square in the Marais, well known to locals but only found by lucky visitors.

The collection itself is scarcely a hundred years old and was amassed by Ernest Cognacq and his wife Louise Jay, who founded the Samaritaine department store in Paris. Paintings by Rembrandt, Rubens, Canaletto, Joshua Reynolds, Watteau and Fragonard, among others, grace the walls. There are also collections of sculpture, porcelain, jewellery and furniture, which concentrate on the French 18th-century arts and contain some magnificent items – though sometimes you have to look closely to spot the gems.

There is very little information in anything other than French so, unless you speak the language reasonably well, your pleasure will depend on your visual appreciation of the objects alone.

Musée National Picasso (6 mins)

Hôtel Salé, 5 rue de Thorigny
***Tel**: (01) 42 71 25 21; www.musee-picasso.fr*
***Open**: May–Sep Wed–Mon 9.30am–6pm, Oct–Apr Wed–Mon 9.30am–5.30pm*
***Adm**: adults €5.50, 18–25s €4, under-18s free, first Sun each month free*

The Picasso Museum in this superb Marais mansion must be in the top ten sights in Paris, if not the top five. Those who only know Picasso from his Cubist and more experimental paintings will uncover a whole new side to his work – that of the

Musée National Picasso

gifted draughtsman, the tender observer and an artist with a great sense of humour.

The building housing the museum, the Hôtel Salé, is also of interest. It was built in the 17th century for a salt-tax collector, hence the name, which means, colloquially, the Salty House.

Work began on the museum in 1976, although it was nine years before it opened. The artist Giacometti designed the furniture and the chandeliers.

The collection is presented in roughly chronological order, although it's easy to skip ahead or to wander back, if you wish. Different visitors will have different highlights, depending on which style and period of Picasso appeals the most, but the artist's self-portrait, painted when he was struggling in poverty in 1901, is especially gripping. *Two Women Running on the Beach* is another favourite; whichever piece catches your eye, you can probably find a reproduction of it in various sizes and printed on various objects in the excellent gift shop – allow time to check it out.

On top of the artist's own work, which extends to ceramics, sculpture and photography, there is a good collection of work Picasso himself acquired, by the artists he most admired, including Matisse, Renoir and Cézanne. There is also a good collection of mainly African tribal art, which so inspired him.

St-Paul-St-Louis (1 min)

99 rue St-Antoine
***Tel**: (01) 42 72 30 32*
***Open**: Sun–Fri 9.30am–7.30pm, Sat 9.30am–12.30pm;*
***Adm**: free*

Going east from the Métro along the main street that runs through the Marais, but often overlooked as visitors head for the place des Vosges (***see*** p.44) and the Marais mansions, is this 17th-century church. Completed in 1641, it became one of the richest in the whole of Paris as the kings of France went to confession here. Louis XIII laid the foundation stone in 1627, and the hearts of Louis XIII and Louis XIV were buried here. After the Revolution many of the church's treasures, including the hearts of the kings, were removed, but one that remains is a painting by Delacroix, *Christ in the Garden of Olives*, and it is this that draws most visitors today.

Hôtel de Sully (2 mins)

62 rue St-Antoine
Tel: *(01) 44 61 20 00*
Open: *courtyard open daily, interior private*

This is one of the most outstanding of the Marais mansions. Although the interior isn't accessible to the general public (unless you happen to have business with the Centre des Monuments Nationaux), you can take a look at the exterior and go into the lovely, honey-coloured courtyard, which canny locals also use as a short cut between the place des Vosges and the rue St-Antoine.

The Hôtel was built in 1624 for a notorious gambler, Petit Thomas, who lost his fortune, including this house, in a single night. In 1634 it was bought by the Duc de Sully, chief minister to Henri IV who put in the orangery. The Hôtel has been wonderfully restored according to the original plans and it is worth having a look at the courtyard whether you need the short cut or not!

Hôtel de Sully

Mémorial de la Shoah (5 mins)

Musée, Centre de Documentation Juive Contemporaine
17 rue Geoffroy l'Asnier; www.memorialdelashoah.fr
***Tel**: 33 1 42 77 44 72;*
***Open**: Sun–Fri 10am–6pm, Thu 10am–10pm*
Closed Sat, national holidays and some Jewish holidays

This brand-new museum and archive, just south of the Métro, opened in January 2005 and is a moving memorial to the Jewish population who died in the Holocaust. It gives access to archived documents, including private letters, photographs, documentary films, and permanent and temporary exhibitions, including Stephen Spielberg's recording of Holocaust survivors recounting their experiences. There is also a programme of children's activities, student tours, public films and lectures. The chilling *Mur des Noms* (Wall of Names) gives a real sense of the statistics of the tragedy, recording the names of all the 76,000 French Jews (11,000 of whom were children) who were deported to Nazi concentration camps between 1942 and 1944; only 2,500 returned home.

BASTILLE

L'Opéra (1 min)

Place de la Bastille
***Tel**: (01) 40 01 19 70 (to book a tour), 08 36 69 78 68 (box office); www.opera-de-paris.fr*
***Open**: daily but pre-booked guided tours only*
***Adm**: tours: adults €10, over-60s €8, under-26s €5*

The full name of the opera building on the place de la Bastille is the Opéra de Paris Bastille, to distinguish it from the old opera house, the Opéra Garnier. The new opera house was officially opened on 14 July 1989, exactly 200 years after the storming of the Bastille Prison which once stood on the far side. The opera house has itself taken a bit of a storming, from critics and audience alike, as the sound was at first said to be very poor (some people still don't like it), and it was beset by problems such as falling tiles.

Today some of the concrete support looks rather distressed, more like a government department than a cutting-edge concert hall. From a distance the building is more impressive, with its curved glass and steel design, and inside there are five moving stages and a great deal of technical wizardry. It is possible to take a tour of the building, but you will need to phone first and get the dates and times of tours in different languages, and book ahead.

Canal St-Martin (1 min)

Place de la Bastille

The Canal St-Martin Right passes right under the place de la Bastille, and it is possible to take a boat trip along it. Boats leave from the Porte de l'Arsenal, which is right alongside, or rather just below, the heavy traffic hurtling around the place de la Bastille. The canal was opened in 1825 and is about 3 miles (5kms) long, running first northwest and then veering northeast, ending up at the Parc de la Villette. The canal passes through several locks and two swing bridges on its way, and is crossed by old-fashioned metal footbridges. A boat trip along the Canal St-Martin is very different from, but just as interesting as, the more popular trips along the River Seine.

Canal St-Martin

Richard Lenoir Market (1 min)

Boulevard Richard Lenoir
***Open**: Thu and Sun mornings*

The markets of Paris are one of the city's delights, and they're fun to stroll around even if you don't think you can pack any of the fresh produce away in your bags to take home. The market at the Bastille end of the boulevard is especially popular on Sundays when weekend visitors mix with the locals, who are there to buy the fresh vegetables, fruit, sweets and other goodies piled high on the colourful stalls.

Rue de Lappe

Rue de Lappe (2 mins)

This is one of the busiest streets for nightlife on the right bank, on the edge of the Bastille area and a two-minute walk northeast from the Métro. As the night gets busier, the narrow street gets more crowded and the noise level increases. If you're at a loose end one evening and fancy a bar but don't know what type, head here as there's sure to be something that appeals to you. There are several good restaurants along here, too, but if you want a quiet meal come early – the bars and nightclubs take over later on.

Rue du Faubourg-St-Antoine (1 min)

This is the main street of the district known as the Faubourg St-Antoine, the word meaning a kind of fake or artificial borough. Not many years ago this was off the map for visitors, a fairly run-down area where there was nothing much to do or see. It has had quite a make-over, though, and began filling with bars, restaurants and fashionable shops. A stroll along the street will show that there is still a mix of the old and the new. Running off the street on both sides are occasional cobbled passageways, down which many furniture workshops still exist. This was once the district's monopolizing trade, and although there are far fewer now than there used to be, the business still flourishes.

La Galoche d'Aurillac

41 rue de Lappe

Tel: (01) 47 00 77 15

Open: Tue–Sat lunch and dinner

Moderate

Wonderful and characterful Auvergne bar–restaurant serving generous helpings of the hearty regional fare, with stuffed cabbage a speciality.

Promenade Plantée (2 mins)

Rue de Lyon/avenue Daumesnil
***Open**: 24 hours*
***Adm**: free*

Just as the Canal St-Martin disappears underground so that most people have no idea what is happening beneath their feet, the Promenade Plantée rises up above the average citizen's head and is totally invisible. Walk past the opera house along the rue de Lyon, and look for steps on your left leading up. There's very little to tell you what mysterious delight is up there, but the promenade is in fact a hidden park. It's a long, thin park – this was once a railway viaduct, but it fell into disuse until a few years ago when the city authorities decided to turn it into a green space.

The Promenade Plantée is extremely popular, and a great place to escape the traffic-filled streets. It runs southeast, and has several points of access. The path zig-zags past flowerbeds and lawns, through arches and into quiet areas with benches where you can enjoy a picnic or read the paper and enjoy the sunshine. You can look down onto the life of the street, and get good views of the apartment buildings as you pass. Eventually the path comes down to ground level again, and will take you all the way to the Bois de Vincennes – providing an attractive alternative to travelling there by Métro.

Viaduc des Arts (2 mins)

Avenue Daumesnil

***Open**: daily, times vary for different shops*

If you continue down the rue de Lyon and follow it round to the avenue Daumesnil, without climbing up to the Promenade Plantée, you will come to the Viaduc des Arts. Just as the top of the viaduct has been transformed by plants, the arches below have been transformed by turning them into art galleries and craft workshops. They range from traditional old furniture and picture restorers to modern jewellery designers and ethnic craft stores, along with a design gallery and the Viaduc Café.

Viaduc Café

43 avenue Daumesnil

Tel: (01) 44 74 70 70

Open: Daily, 9am–4am, food served lunch and dinner only

Inexpensive

Underneath the arches of the former railway line, and now the Promenade Plantée, you can drop in just to have a drink, or to have a full meal in the bar, on the terrace or in the restaurant. It's a lot larger than it looks from outside, and is relaxed and stylish.

Place des Vosges (4 mins)

The place des Vosges is one of the loveliest squares in Paris, although it wasn't always as attractive as it is today. It went out of fashion for a time and became rather run down, before it was transformed in a recent regeneration programme. It is now restored to its original elegance when it was constructed almost 400 years ago. The square was designed in 1612 and it was the first time that arcades and balconies had been used between buildings in Paris in this way. The initial intention was that the whole square would be a silk factory, with

Arcade, Place des Voges

housing for its workers, but this plan was never implemented, and the square quickly became one of the most sought-after addresses in Paris.

Over the centuries some famous people have lived here, including Victor Hugo, Molière, Cardinal Richelieu and Madame de Sévigné, who was born here. However, the square began to decay when the court moved to Versailles in 1686, and many of the wealthy people who could afford an address in the place des Vosges moved with them. It wasn't until as recently as the 1960s that the whole of the Marais was made into a historic district, at first protected and then regenerated.

Maison de Victor Hugo (4 mins)

Hôtel de Rohan-Guéménée, 6 place des Vosges
***Tel**: (01) 42 72 10 16*
***Open**: Tue–Sun 10am–6pm*
***Adm**: adults €5.60, students €4, 13–26s €2.50, under-13s free*

This, the largest private house on the prestigious place des Vosges, is where the highly prolific and highly revered French author Victor Hugo lived from 1832 until 1848. It was during this period that he wrote one of his best-known works, Les Misérables. The house is now a museum in Hugo's honour, with reconstructions of some of the rooms as they were in his day, along with editions of his work, manuscripts, drawings and photographs – Hugo was fascinated by the world of photography, which was developing in the later years of his life.

There are also rooms reconstructed from other houses where Hugo lived, and the room in which he died in 1885. Some of the furniture was made by Hugo himself. Even if you are not particularly interested in Hugo, it is worth visiting the museum to get an idea of the life of someone at the nub of Parisian literary life in the mid-19th century, when fellow writers, including Dumas, climbed those same stone steps that lead up to Hugo's apartments.

Montmartre

LINE 2

PORTE DAUPHINE – NATION

Line 2 opened five months after Line 1, on 13 December 19[illegible] Despite its name, it was not the second line, which was line (*see* p.82) and was just a short two-stop hop via place Victor Hugo and Porte Dauphine. However, less than three years lat[illegible] it had been extended in a rough semi-circle through northe[illegible] Paris, so that it eventually linked up again with Line 1 at Natio[illegible] its eastern end. It's one of the quieter lines for visitors as it doesn't go through the city centre and, along its length of 12.3km (7.7 miles), you'll see some of the variety of suburban Paris, from the well-heeled to down-at-heel.

CHARLES DE GAULLE ÉTOILE

Arc de Triomphe, *see* p.14

TERNES

Alexandre Nevsky Cathedral 48

COURCELLES

MONCEAU

Parc Monceau 49

Musée Cernuschi 49

Musée Nissim de Camondo 50

VILLIERS

ROME

PLACE DE CLICHY

BLANCHE

Moulin Rouge 51

Cimetière de Montmartre 51

Musée de l'Érotisme 52

Montmartre 53

PIGALLE

Place Pigalle 54

ANVERS

Sacré-Coeur 54

See also Line 12, **Lamarck-Caulaincourt, p.156**

Au Lapin Agile p.156, Montmartre Vineyards p.157, Musée de Montmartre p.157, Avenue Junot p.158, Moulin de la Galette p.159

See also **Line 12, Abbesses, p159**

Place des Abbesses p.159

St-Jean l'Évangéliste de Montmartre p.160, Espace Montmartre Salvador Dali p.161, Place du Tertre p.162, St-Pierre de Montmartre p.163

BARBÈS ROCHECHOUART

LA CHAPELLE

STALINGRAD

JAURÈS

Canal St-Martin, ***see*** p.41

COLONEL FABIEN

BELLEVILLE

COURONNES

Musée Edith Piaf 57

PÈRE-LACHAISE

Père-Lachaise Cemetery 58

CHARLES DE GAULLE ÉTOILE

***See* Line 1, p.14**
Arc de Triomphe p.14

TERNES

Alexandre Nevsky Cathedral (2 mins)

12 rue Daru
***Tel**: (01) 42 27 37 34*
***Open**: Tue, Fri and Sun 3–5pm*
***Adm**: free*

Paris's Russian Orthodox Cathedral is a striking sight, its onion domes not something you expect to see on the city's skyline, although there has been a sizeable Russian population in Paris for some time. This was boosted after the Russian Revolution when many citizens fled to the safety of Paris, and the welcome given by this cathedral. It was completed in 1861, having taken two years to build, and is in what was then and remains today, the Russian quarter with Russian tea shops, delis, clothing stores, bookshops and other outlets. Opening hours are limited, but there are still services on Sunday.

Brasserie Lorraine

2–4 place des Ternes

Tel: (01) 56 21 22 00

Open: daily noon–12.30am

Expensive

Brasserie that specializes in seafood, which can be expensive, but you could stick to a plate of oysters and a glass of wine to set you up for more sightseeing.

Alexandre Nevsky Cathedral

MONCEAU

Parc Monceau

Le Clou

132 rue Cardinet

Tel: (01) 42 27 36 78

Open: Mon–Fri lunch and dinner, Sat dinner

Moderate

A bit of a walk north from the Métro (the Malesherbes station is slightly closer) but worth it for this usually crowded and lively bistro whose quality belies the price, especially if you go for the bargain fixed-price lunch menu.

Parc Monceau (1 mins)

Boulevard de Courcelles
***Open**: daily, dawn–dusk*
***Adm**: free*

Monceau is a very well-heeled area of Paris and the park is a peaceful oasis of gentility northwest of the city centre. It used to be even bigger – part of it was sold off in 1852 to allow the building of some luxurious houses, which can still be seen today. In 1861 it was turned into a public park.

The Duke of Chartres originally created this park in 1778 as a garden on what was then the open Monceau Plain. The designer, a writer and artist named Carmontelle, was heavily influenced by the English and German landscaped gardens that were popular during that period and designed the gardens accordingly. They were, and are, filled with follies, ruins and whimsical buildings, wrought-iron gates and a pond in the shape of a tree. There are lots of real trees, too, and numerous statues hidden around the grounds, including monuments to Guy de Maupassant, Chopin and other leading writers and musicians of the late 19th century. In contrast with the high art there are also swings, roundabouts and donkey rides for children.

Musée Cernuschi (2 mins)

7 avenue Velasquez
***Tel**: (01) 45 63 50 75; www.paris.fr/musees*
***Open**: Tue–Sun 10am–5.40pm*
***Adm**: free*

Admirers of Asian art should make for this lovely museum, which houses a fine collection of some 10,000 items. The original collection consisted of 5000 or so objects that were amassed by Enrico Cernuschi, a wealthy Italian banker and politician. Most of them were collected astonishingly, on one 18-month trip to the Far East that began in 1871, concentrating on China and Japan. The paintings, statues, pottery, jade, jewellery and other items were then put on display in Cernuschi's lavish mansion near Parc Monceau.

When he died in 1896, Cernuschi bequeathed his collection to the city of Paris. Highlights include a bronze vase dating from the 12th century BC, a 5th century Buddha and some exquisite 8th century paintings of horses on silk by the court artist Han Kan who was one of the masters of the art form.

Musée Nissim de Camondo (3 mins)

63 rue de Monceau
***Tel**: (01) 53 89 06 40; www.ucad.fr*
***Open**: Wed–Sun 10am–5pm*
***Adm**: adults €4.60, 18–25s €3.10,under-18s free*

The building housing this fine art collection is more modern than some that are in the area, having been built in 1914 as a copy of the Petit Trianon at Versailles, Marie-Antoinette's favourite little château (***see*** p.179). This mansion, however, was built for a rich Jewish financier, the Comte Moïse de Camondo, specifically to house his superb collection of 16th-century fine art objects, including tapestries, paintings, furniture and other items.

Nissim was the first name of the Comte's son who died in action during World War I. When the Comte died in 1935, he bequeathed the house and collection to the French state on condition that it was named after Nissim Camondo. Tragically, the Comte's daughter and her family were all killed at the concentration camp in Auschwitz less than ten years later.

Highlights of the collection include a vase, which was once owned by Marie-Antoinette, carpets, fine furniture made by craftsmen to the royal families and collections of the finest porcelain. Some of the rooms, including the Comte's bedroom and the kitchens, have been restored to give a glimpse of the upstairs–downstairs life in the mansion when this was the Comte's own home.

Moulin Rouge

BLANCHE

Moulin Rouge (1 min)

82 boulevard de Clichy
***Tel**: (01) 53 09 82 82; www.moulin-rouge.com*
***Open**: daily, dinner at 7pm and shows at 9pm and 11pm*
***Adm**: €82–160*

It's not difficult to spot the Moulin Rouge along the, sometimes sleazy, boulevard de Clichy. Just look for the trademark red windmill, which is what the name means. However, the world-famous home of the can-can dancers has never had a real windmill on the site, apart from the one on the roof, which is for publicity purposes. It borrows the name from other windmills that used to exist further up on the slopes of Montmartre, a one-time hilly village outside of Paris (***see*** p.53).

The Moulin Rouge opened its doors in 1889 with shows featuring the can-can girls, and other scantily clad dancers, some of whom were immortalized in the publicity posters made for the Moulin by Toulouse-Lautrec. Some of these can be seen today in the Musée d'Orsay (***see*** p.165), a far cry from their rather disreputable origins. The shows still go on, of course, at a price, and for some visitors are an essential part of Paris by night.

Le Wepier

14 place de Clichy

Tel: (01) 45 22 53 24; www.welper.com

Open: daily noon–1am

Moderate

Five minutes from Blanche, this is an archetypal, big and busy French brasserie with the usual comprehensive menu, where you can eat simply or fancily, depending on your mood and your budget.

Cimetière de Montmartre (2 mins)

20 avenue Rachel
***Tel**: (01) 43 87 64 24*
***Open**: Mar–Nov Mon–Fri 8am–6pm, Sat 8.30am–6pm, Sun and hols 9am–6pm (Nov–Mar closes 5.30pm)*
***Adm**: free; tours available, call ahead for times and booking*

The cemetery at Montmartre opened in 1798 and is perhaps second only to Père-Lachaise as a resting place for the famous. Once you find the entrance (there are stairs from rue Caulaincourt), you can easily spend an hour or two tracking down the best-known graves, or just enjoying the greenery and seeing some of the oddities that any graveyard produces.

One grave that's unmissable near the entrance, is that of the 19th-century French icon, author Emile Zola, although the grave is all that remains as the author's body was transferred to the Panthéon in 1908. Zola was famous for writing books based on social reality, such as *Nana* (1880), about a prostitute and *Germinal* (1885), which was highly critical of working conditions down the mines. Oher names to look for include Hector Berlioz, Heinrich Heine, François Truffaut, Edgar Degas, Offenbach, Nijinsky, Alexandre Dumas *fils*, Georges Feydeau and the writer Stendhal, by his name of Henry Beyle. If you have just visited the Moulin Rouge (***see*** p.51) you might want to look for the grave of one of its most famous dancers, La Goulue (Louise Weber), who appeared in the posters by Toulouse-Lautrec and was one of the cabaret's first can-can stars. Her grave is close to that of Emile Zola, on the far side of the roundabout.

Musée de l'Érotisme (1 min)

72 boulevard de Clichy
***Tel**: (01) 42 58 28 73; www.eroticmuseum.com*
***Open**: daily 10am–2am*
***Adm**: adults €7, students €5*

You'd be forgiven for thinking that the Erotic Museum would be a cheap and tawdry tourist rip-off exploiting the local sex industry, or something for the dirty-mac brigade that you should shy away from. Not a bit of it. It's a bright and modern, well-organized and well-displayed museum, far more fascinating than some subjects that have museums devoted to them. It was opened in 1998 when co-owner Alain Plumey joined with some friends to put his collection of over 5,000 erotic items on public display. And a fascinating collection it is, of paintings, dolls, fetishes, statues, photographs, toys, writings, ceramics, automata – just about anything you can imagine, and a few things you probably can't. It's not for the prudish, but it certainly isn't something to hurry past if you're genuinely interested.

Montmartre (7 mins)

If there is one area of Paris that conjures up most people's idea of the city, then it's Montmartre. Perhaps a city that no longer exists, of struggling artists and not-so-struggling showgirls, but an image of Paris that many of us carry with us and will always be in the mind. That Paris did exist, in the streets of the hilly village of Montmartre, in the late 19th century and the early days of the 20th century. Artists like Van Gogh, Toulouse-Lautrec, Picasso, Utrillo and others did live there, did paint there, were poor and took on menial jobs sometimes in order to survive. Cabarets and clubs like the **Moulin Rouge** (*see* p.51) and **Au Lapin Agile** (*see* p.156) started up around the same time, contributing to the Bohemian lifestyle – and still survive.

Montmartre survives, too, perhaps more than you might imagine. There is still a distinct feel to it, as if you are in a specia part of Paris. The hilly, cobbled streets can take your breath away in more ways than one. Even a **vineyard** (*see* p.157) still clings on, the only one in Paris, and only in Montmartre can you imagine people harvesting the vines, bottling the wine, and having a party to celebrate the vintage. You won't find the real Montmartre in the **place du Tertre**

Montmartre

(*see* p.162), where today's artists hang out making lightning sketches of the visitors, but if you venture away from there and wander the streets you'll certainly be rewarded. The sights below at Pigalle and Anvers are all in the area.

See also Line 12 for stations, Lamarck-Caulaincourt p.156 and Abbesses p.159.

PIGALLE

Place Pigalle (1 min)

In Paris the name Pigalle has long gone hand in hand with sex and sleaze. It still does, but the area is changing. Just as the Soho of London was transformed, there is an attempt to clean up the streets around Pigalle, get rid of the streetwalkers and close down the more offensive strip shows and sex shops. There is a long way still to go, but it is starting to happen. In any case, much of the larger area of Pigalle is perfectly pleasant. Walk a few blocks south of place Pigalle and you are in a neighbourhood like any other, of street markets and patisseries, bars and bistros. Place Pigalle itself is worth a quick look, but you will soon want to head south into Pigalle or north into Montmartre (*see* p.53) and up to Sacré-Coeur (*see* p.54).

La Fourmi

74 rue des Martyrs

Tel: (01) 42 64 70 35

Open: Mon–Thu 8am–2am, Fri–Sat 8am–4am, Sun 10am–2am, food served daily noon–11pm

Walking time: 1 min

Inexpensive

You can get a drink here almost 24 hours a day, and food most of the day. The Fourmi is the modern equivalent of the old Montmartre hang-outs, with its traditional zinc bar, smoky atmosphere and customers who look as arty as they come.

ANVERS

Sacré-Coeur (7 mins)

35 rue du Chevalier-de-la-Barre
Tel*: (01) 53 41 89 00*
Open*: daily 6am–10.30pm*
Adm*: free (admission fee to crypt and dome)*

One of the best views of Paris is to be had from the front of the basilica of the Sacré-Coeur. You will probably have to share it with dozens if not hundreds of other people, though, as this church, on the eastern edge of Montmartre is on every first-time visitor's and coach-party itinerary but it doesn't stop it being special.

Sacré Coeur

It's a bit of a climb from the Métro at Anvers, although there is also a funicular (use one Métro ticket) for those who prefer not to walk. It's a pleasant walk up, through greenery, and for most of the way, is a fairly gentle incline, giving an impressive view of the front of the church as you near the top.

The church is over the top in many ways. It has had plenty of critics over the years, with people likening it to a wedding cake and calling it a monstrosity, but it's a monstrosity that has survived and its distinctive shape is now as strongly associated with Paris as the Eiffel Tower, Notre-Dame or the Arc de Triomphe.

The origins of the church go back to 1870, and the start of the Franco-Prussian War. France was expected to be walked over by the might of the Prussian army, and two Catholic businessmen, Alexandre Legentil and Rohault de Fleury, agreed that they would build a church to the honour of the Sacred Heart if France was spared. France was spared the feared carnage and, despite a long siege, Paris was not invaded, so work on the church began in 1875. It was completed in 1914, but because of World War I it wasn't consecrated until 1919.

The church's great dome is the second highest point on the Paris skyline, after the Eiffel Tower (***see*** p.87), and can be visited. It is open during the day (small fee) and you can climb almost to the top, from where you can see for over 30kms (18 miles) on a clear day. There's also a wonderful view back down into the church itself. Down in the crypt (small fee), there is an audiovisual display on the history of the church, which quickly became a place of pilgrimage, and there's also an urn containing the heart of one of the founders, Alexandre Legentil.

At the back of the Sacré-Coeur is another of its outstanding features: the belltower. This stands some 83m (252ft) high and is renowned for containing one of the heaviest bells in the world. Known as *La Savoyarde*, because it was a gift from the Catholics of the Savoy region, it weighs almost 19 tonnes.

See also Line 12, Lamarck-Caulaincourt, p.156

Au Lapin Agile p.156, Montmartre Vineyards p.157, Musée de Montmartre p.157, Avenue Junot p.158, Moulin de la Galette p.159

See also Line 12, Abbesses, p.159

Place des Abbesses p.159, St-Jean l'Évangéliste de Montmartre p.160, Espace Montmartre Salvador Dali p.161, Place du Tertre p.162, St-Pierre de Montmartre p.163

Musée Edith Piaf (3 mins)

5 rue Crespin-du-Gast
***Tel**: (01) 43 55 52 72*
***Open**: by appointment only, Mon–Wed 1–6pm, Thu 9am–noon, Jun and Sep closed*
***Adm**: donation requested*

There are several reasons for visiting this museum, not least that it takes you out to Belleville, a part of Paris to which few visitors venture, although it's a fascinating, culturally mixed part of the city. Another reason is the nature of the museum, which occupies two rooms and can only be visited by appointment.

The museum is run by *Les Amis d'Edith Piaf* (the Friends of Edith Piaf), a group of enthusiasts dedicated to keeping the memory of Paris's favourite singer alive. The 'little sparrow', as she was known, has a special place in the hearts of older Parisians, familiar with her tough upbringing, her tiny frame, her unique voice and the uncompromising nature and passion she put into songs like 'Je ne regrette rien' ('I regret nothing').

She was born in the area, although probably not under a lamp post as legend has it and it was here, as well as around Pigalle (***see*** p.54) that she sang in squares and on street corners before she became a public success. She died to great public grief in 1963 and is buried in the Père Lachaise cemetery (***see*** p.58).

Here you can see just how little the little sparrow was, as her black dress and shoes seem almost doll-sized. There are the other items you would expect, such as movie and theatre posters, photographs, letters and some personal memorabilia, but the very small scale of the place, and its human size, bring the person of Piaf home to the visitor in a way that bigger enterprises sometimes fail to do. Definitely one of Paris's little delights.

PÈRE-LACHAISE

Cimetière de Père-Lachaise (1 min)

Boulevard de Ménilmontant
Tel: *(01) 55 25 82 10*
Open: *Mar–Nov Mon–Fri 8am–6pm, Sat 8.30am–6pm, Sun and hols 9am–6pm (Nov–Mar closes 5.30pm)*
Adm: *free*

Paris's largest cemetery has become a tourist attraction in its own right, and not just for its amazing array of famous people buried within its 40 hectares (almost 100 acres). Many of the lesser-known graves are impressive monuments, and the collection of statuary inside its walls can sometimes seem to rival that of any museum or gallery. In addition, the sloping cobbled pathways, the tree-lined avenues and the wildlife can make a visit seem like a pleasant stroll in a park. It is certainly an impressive resting place for those buried here. A map of the cemetery is useful (www.paris.org/Expos/PereLachaise/pl.history.html).

Père-Lachaise was never intended only to be a cemetery. It was always planned to be a rural space as well, which people could enjoy visiting. It was designed in 1804 and named after Père de la Chaise, a Jesuit who had been the confessor to King Louis XIV in the 17th century. The site was originally owned by de la Chaise, and there was a home for retired priests here that he was fond of visiting.

When it later opened as a cemetery bearing his name, the site very quickly became known as the burial place for the famous and sometimes the infamous. This was helped by the fact that some graves, including that of Molière, were actually moved here for what we now might call PR purposes.

Today the cemetery needs little PR help, as its roll-call of residents attracts visitors from all over the world – and are not always welcome, particularly the fans of the Doors singer Jim Morrison, who come to decorate his grave but sadly occasionally

Ma Pomme

107 rue de Ménilmontant

Tel: (01) 40 33 10 40

Open: Mon–Fri lunch, Mon–Sat dinner, first Sat each month 11am–2am

Inexpensive–moderate

Great food at good prices in this sumptuously decorated restaurant. It's a 10-minute walk from the Métro and the cemetery, but a walk worth making.

desecrate the graves around by their behaviour. Admirers visit the graves of many writers who are buried here – Oscar Wilde who died alone and penniless in Paris in 1900, the French authors Colette, Balzac, Proust and Appollinaire, the American writer Gertrude Stein and poet Richard Wright – and others in the arts such as Rossini, Delacroix, Corot, Géricault, Modigliani, Baron Haussman, Chopin, Sarah Bernhardt, Yves Montand, Simone Signoret, Isadors Duncan, Maria Callas and Edith Piaf (***see*** p.57).

There are so many graves here, of the famous and less well known, and the cemetery is so big, that it is best to get yourself a map rather than wander around randomly. You can get one from the cemetery office by the main entrance gates, or buy one from shops in the cemetery. Some of the companies who organize walking tours of Paris include Père-Lachaise on their itineraries.

Tomb of composer Frédéric Chopin, Père-Lachaise Cemetery

Notre-Dame

LINE 4

PORTE DE CLIGNANCOURT – PORTE D'ORLÉANS

Line 4 extends from north to south and goes under the Seine with a stop on the Île de la Cité along the way – a route that caused major engineering problems. To make it possible, the line was opened in stages. In April 1908 the northern section opened, running from the suburbs of Porte de Clignancourt to Les Halles, just north of the river at Châtelet. In October 1909 the first southern section was completed, from Porte d'Orléans as far as Raspail, still some way out of the centre. By January 1910 the two sections had been joined. It has always been the busiest of all the Métro lines.

LES HALLES

Les Halles (0 mins)

***Open**: daily, shop hours vary*

Bang in the centre of Paris is the area known as Les Halles. Like London's Covent Garden, Les Halles was both a city district and the old food market, which had been there since 1183. Also, like Covent Garden in the 1960s, it had to move from its central position to the outskirts because the narrow streets around it couldn't support the volume of heavy traffic delivering to and from the market (*Les Halles* is the word for a covered market area). The site was redeveloped into a huge shopping centre in 1979 with hundreds of shops, and facilities such as a swimming pool, cinema, cultural centres and rooftop gardens. Controversy has always raged over the 1960s design and in 2004 the decision was made to tear the whole thing down and start all over again. Whether you like it or not, it's a vibrant area and part of historical Paris – look out for **Rue de la Ferronerie** where Henri IV was assassinated in 1610, the **place J. du Bellay**, home to the Fontaine des Innocents, the last-surviving Renaissance fountain in Paris and the **Rue Quincampoix**, lined with lovely 18th-century buildings. East of the Métro, you will find the **Centre Georges Pompidou** (***see** p.148*).

Les Halles

Pharamond

24 rue de la Grande-Truanderie

Tel: (01) 40 28 45 18; www.le-pharamond.com

Open: Mon–Sat lunch and dinner

Moderate

This Normandy restaurant is also an historical site, built as it was in 1832 and with its ornate Art Nouveau interior intact. The menu goes for lots of pork, butter, cream, cider and of course Calvados.

Église St-Eustache (3 mins)

Rue du Jour
***Tel**: (01) 40 26 47 99*
***Open**: daily 9am–7.30pm*
***Adm**: free*

St-Eustache is heavenly; it is one of the most beautiful churches in Paris and second only to Notre-Dame in size, upon which it is based, with double aisles, five naves and several side chapels. Not surprisingly, it took 105 years to build, from 1532 to 1637, at a time when Renaissance architecture was flourishing – although the plan was Gothic, the decoration is Renaissance at its best.

Église St-Eustache

Au Pied de Cochon

6 rue Coquillière

Tel: (01) 40 13 77 00; www.pieddecochon.com

Open: daily, 24 hours

Moderate

The name means the pig's foot, and that's the signature dish, although there are plenty of other brasserie-style dishes on offer too, in this place that never closes.

There has been a church on this site since at least 1214, when a chapel is known to have been built here, originally dedicated to St Agnes but later re-dedicated to St Eustache, a Roman general who converted to Christianity. He is said to have seen a vision of the cross between the antlers of a stag, which is why you will find a stag's head and cross carved into the church's façade. St Eustache was later martyred, roasted alive with his wife and children inside a bronze bull.

Partly because of the market, and also its central position, the district of Les Halles became one of the biggest and crowded in Paris, and the old church of St-Eustache became too small to cope, so the present one was planned. It is because the plans were so ambitious that there were 105 years between commencement and consecration.

Many events have taken place here over the years, including the baptism of Cardinal Richelieu, the world premières of Berlioz's *Te Deum* and the *Grand Mass* by Liszt, and the burial of Molière – although he was later moved to Père-Lachaise (***see*** p.58). The organ is notable for having some 8,000 pipes, one of the largest in the world. To hear how it sounds you can attend a free recital on Sundays for half an hour at 5.30pm.

Other highlights include a painting by Rubens, *Pilgrims at Emmaus*, and a charming carved scene near the rear of the church interior depicting some of the workers from the old market at Les Halles, for whom this was their parish church.

Centre Georges Pompidou, *see* Rambuteau, p.148

CITÉ (ÎLE DE LA CITÉ)

Flower Market *(Marché aux Fleurs)* (1 min)

Place Louis-Lépine, quai des Fleurs
***Open**: daily, all day*

Paris is full of markets, but perhaps none is as colourful and fragrant as the Flower Market on the northern side of the Île de la Cité. Weekend mornings are usually the busiest time. Parisians love flowers. They decorate their homes with them and they grow them in the tiniest space in a window box or on a balcony. There are stalls that specialize in orchids, others in herbs, and there are also a few fixed greenhouses with heady exotic plants. On Sunday the live-bird market moves in, though there are still some flower stalls then, too.

Flower Market

La Conciergerie (2 mins)

1 quai de l'Horloge
***Tel**: (01) 53 40 60 97*
***Open**: Apr–Sep daily 9.30am–6.30pm, Oct–Mar daily 9am–5pm*
***Adm**: adults €6.10 students and 12–25s €4.10, under-12s free*

Best known for being a prison during the time of the French Revolution, and the place where Marie-Antoinette was held before her execution (you can still see the tiny cell), the Conciergerie is a fascinating slice of Paris history. It isn't one of the city's best-known sites, but is definitely worth the price of admission.

Best seen from the river, the building is part of the Palais de Justice and its unusual

La Conciergerie

name is due to the fact that it was once the home of the *Comte des Cierges* (Count of the Candles), so-called because he was in charge of lodgings for the royal palace, as well as taxes. It's where *concierge* comes from. He became the chief gaoler when the offices became a prison, although there had always been dungeons in these buildings, which once housed the royal palace.

In 1793–4, at the height of the Revolution, it is said that 2,600 prisoners passed through La Conciergerie on their way to a date with Madame Guillotine, including Queen Marie-Antoinette who, according to popular legend, had said of the starving Paris peasants, 'let them eat cake'. She stayed here for three months before meeting her execution.

There's more to the visit than just seeing the cells, fascinating though they are. There is also the *Salles des Gens d'Armes* (Hall of the Men-at-Arms), a vast chamber where concerts are now held. You can also visit the 14th-century kitchens, where feasts for up to 3,000 people were once prepared.

Sainte-Chapelle (2 mins)

4 boulevard du Palais
***Tel**: (01) 53 40 60 97*
***Open**: Apr–Sep daily 9.30am–6.30pm, Oct–Mar daily 10am–5pm*
***Adm**: adults €6.10, students and 12–25s €4.10, under-12s free*

To walk inside the upper tier of the church of Sainte-Chapelle for the first time is to have one of the most glorious experiences

Sainte-Chapelle

in Paris. Especially so if the day is sunny, because this one church has a greater area of stained glass than any church in the world, all the more effective for being housed in a comparatively small building.

The Sainte-Chapelle, or Holy Chapel, was built in 1248 by Louis IX, or St Louis, the only French king to have been canonized. It was constructed to house the relics he had brought back from his first crusade, which included the Crown of Thorns, a nail from the cross and drops of Christ's blood. St Louis paid more for the relics than it cost to build the church in which they were displayed.

The church has survived better than the relics did (though the Crown of Thorns is now at Notre-Dame, ***see*** below), despite considerable damage during the Revolution when some of its gold was melted down. Fortunately, the magnificent stained glass survived. When you enter the ground floor chapel, where the members of the royal court prayed, you might wonder what the fuss is about as this is a darker area; it is when you make your way up the narrow stairs to the upper chapel, where the royal family prayed, that the unique nature of this church becomes instantly evident.

There are about 1,500 square metres of glass, telling the story of the Bible in 1134 separate scenes. The easiest thing is simply to let your gaze wander and admire the scenes that are best illuminated. These change with the seasons, weather and time of day, but whenever it is that first look will take your breath away.

Le Vieux Bistro

14 rue du Cloître-Notre-Dame

Tel: (01) 43 54 18 95

Open: daily lunch and dinner

Moderate

Right by Notre-Dame, a location that in most places would mean a tourist rip-off, Le Vieux Bistro serves excellent bistro food at reasonable prices and will have as many Parisians as visitors packed inside.

Notre-Dame (2 mins)

Place du Parvis-Notre-Dame
***Tel**: (01) 42 34 56 10*
***Open**: Mon–Fri 8am–6.45pm, Sat–Sun 8am–7.45pm*
***Adm**: free (charge to visit towers)*

The foundation stone of this magnificent monument was laid in 1163, and thousands of craftsmen laboured for 170 years to create the cathedral of Notre-Dame (Our Lady), the spiritual heart not just of the capital city but of the whole of France. Your first sight of it, whether the awe-inspiring entrance on the west front, or the outline against the sky from down below on the river, is a thrilling moment, akin to seeing the Eiffel Tower (***see** p.87*) Paris's other iconic building, for the first time.

That foundation stone was laid by Pope Alexander III (which means it was very important!) and it was designed by Bishop Maurice de Sully. A particular feature was the use of the flying buttresses, which allowed higher and thinner walls than had been built before, adding to the feeling of height, of grandeur and of spaciousness. The best examples are on the eastern façade. You can get a good view of the buttresses from square Jean XXIII, behind the cathedral.

The western façade is the cathedral's 'best side', however. Originally covered with beautiful Gothic statues and carvings of Biblical scenes, the statues were restored in the 19th centruy after many of them were destroyed during the Revolution.

Outside the cathedral, look up and you will see its famous gargoyles, familiar to anyone who knows the story of Victor Hugo's novel, *The Hunchback of Notre-Dame,* published in 1813. If it wasn't for the French author, Notre-Dame might not be still standing there today. It had been crumbling over the years and, even for the crowning of the Emperor Napoleon in 1804, parts of it were in a sorry state and had to be hidden with wall hangings and other disguises. Hugo was determined to save it, and ran a successful campaign to have it restored to its former great glory.

Other famous people associated with the building include Joan of Arc, who was found not guilty of heresy at a trial here in 1455. Unfortunately, she had already been burned at the stake some 24 years previously. Charles I of England was married here, and Henry VI of England was crowned here in 1430, as he also claimed the throne of

Notre Dame

France and in 1559, Mary Queen of Scots was also crowned here as Queen to the French King François II.

One highlight of Notre-Dame is the north *Rose window*, the only one of the three rose windows in the cathedral to retain its original 13th-century stained glass. The *Treasury* contains what is claimed to be a piece of the true cross and the crown of thorns (***see*** Sainte-Chapelle p.65), but they are only displayed once a year, on Good Friday. Visitors can pay a small fee to climb the 387 steps up to the north tower, which is 69m (226ft) high and offers quite a view, once you have your breath back.

The *Archaeological Crypt*, entered from the square in front of the cathedral, is France's 'Point Zéro', the distance from which all measurements throughout France are taken. When something is 857 kilometres from Paris, it's measured from this spot.

Les Bouchons de François Clerc

12 rue de l'Hôtel Colbert

Tel: (01) 43 54 15 34; www.lesbouchonsdefrancoisclerc.com

Open: Mon–Fri lunch and diner, Sat dinner

Moderate

Another Paris eating place that's worth visiting for the setting, housed as it is in an 18th-century mansion. It has superior food without running into the *haute cuisine* prices, and look out for others around the city as this is now one of a small chain.

ST-MICHEL

Boulevard St-Michel (1 min)

South from the Métro, away from the river is the boulevard St-Michel, or 'Boul'Mich' as many Parisians call it. It's been here since 1869, and in the 1960s was a hotbed of student activity, sitting as it does in the middle of the Latin Quarter, the Left Bank and the Sorbonne University. These days it is still lively – an intellectual and arty area of bookshops, poetry readings, nightlife, café discussions and clothes shops.

St-Séverin (1 min)

1 rue des Prêtres-St-Séverin
***Tel**: (01) 42 34 93 50*
***Open**: Mon, Thu–Sat 11am–7.30pm, Tue–Wed 11am–10pm, Sun 9am–8.30pm*
***Adm**: free*

The church of St-Séverin is not one of the best known in Paris but is one of the most visually striking, and is the official church for the University of Paris. It's regarded as the city's best example of Flamboyant Gothic, and a text-book example of what the phrase actually means. St Séverin was a 6th-century hermit, and the church bearing his name was built around 1220; apart from its architectural style, the church is noted for some fine modern stained glass and its 18th-century organ, on which both Fauré and Saint-Saëns have played.

St-Séverin

St-Julien-le-Pauvre (2 mins)

Rue St-Julien-le-Pauvre
Tel: *(01) 43 54 52 16*
Open: *Mon–Sat 9.30am–noon and 3–6.30pm, Sun 9.30am–6.30pm*
Adm: *free*

St Julian the Poor was a 3rd-century bishop who gave all his money to the poor. Founded in 1165, this church which was built in his honour, can claim to be the oldest in Paris. The church of St-Germain-des-Prés (***see*** p.73) is older, but it didn't stand within the city walls. St-Julien-le-Pauvre has had two major restorations and, although it's not the most attractive of Paris's churches, it is of considerable historic interest. Not long after it was built, Pierre Abélard left Notre-Dame and established a new university here, bringing 3,000 students with him. This church is thus home of Paris University.

La Rôtisserie d'en Face

2 rue Christine

Tel: (01) 43 26 40 98; www.jacques-cagna.com

Open: Mon–Fri lunch and dinner, Sat dinner

Moderate

Across the street from the gourmet temple of Michelin-starred chef Jacques Cagna is this more affordable bistro. The food here is simpler and cheaper, but still of a superb quality and highly recommended if you've time to linger and enjoy it.

Musée de Cluny, *see* Cluny La Sorbonne, p.136

ODÉON

Le Procope (2 mins)

13 rue de l'Ancienne-Comédie
Tel: *(01) 43 26 99 20*
Open: *daily 11am–midnight*

Founded in 1686, this is the oldest café in Paris; and through its doors have passed such disparate names as Voltaire, Balzac, Victor Hugo, Rousseau, Napoleon Bonaparte, Benjamin Franklin, Thomas Jefferson, Simone de Beauvoir and Jean-Paul Sartre. It became a restaurant in the 1950s, though if you peek inside you'll see that the décor still dates back to the 18th century.

Restaurant sign, Le Procope

Les Editeurs

4 carrefour de l'Odéon

Tel: (01) 43 26 67 76; www.lesediteurs.fr

Open: daily from 8am, food from noon–2am

Moderate

The name comes from the many publishers' offices that are round about, and many editors hang out here, either for coffee or for the food that ranges from simple and cheap to quite fancy and not quite so cheap.

Alcazar

62 rue Mazarine

Tel: (01) 53 10 19 99; www.alcazar.fr

Open: Daily, lunch and dinner

Moderate

This place caused a stir as it was here that Englishman Terence Conran dared to open a restaurant in the French capital. A roaring success. Alcazar is noted for its fish dishes, although it has plenty of other items on the menu. There's a bar upstairs if you only want a drink and to take a look at this fashionable hang-out.

Cour du Commerce St-André (1 min)

This courtyard tucked away to the north of the Métro has one curious historical claim to fame. It was at no.9 that one Dr Guillotin lived, who came up with the idea of an execution device that was relatively humane, as it brought death instantaneously … most of the time. Another doctor, Dr Louis, perfected the mechanics of the machine and when it was used during the French Revolution it was not called a 'Guillotine' but a 'Louisette'.

Cour de Rohan (1 min)

It's the back streets of Paris that hide its secrets, like these courtyards right by the Cour du Commerce St-André, which date back to the 15th century when they were part of the home of the archbishops of Rouen, later corrupted to Rohan. The central of the three courtyards has an iron block known as a *pas-de-mule*, which was used by anyone who needed a help getting on their mules. It is the only one left in Paris.

Musée de la Monnaie de Paris (5 mins)

11 quai de Conti
***Tel**: (01) 40 46 55 35; www.monnaiedeparis.fr*
***Open**: Tue–Fri 11am–5.30pm, Sat–Sun noon–5.30pm*
***Adm**: adults €3, students €2.20, under-16s and over-60s free, and free first Sun of each month*

A museum about money might not sound too thrilling, but this provides a fascinating journey through the story of French money, starting in Roman times and continuing to the euro, with all its sophisticated security and printing techniques. Many note designs are beautiful when viewed in close detail with time to linger over and appreciate them. The museum is housed in Paris's mint, dating from the 1770s, a lovely building in its own right.

Rue de l'Odéon (1 min)

In the traffic and crowds of a modern city like Paris one can overlook the beauty of the buildings on streets like this. It was

Rue de l'Odéon

constructed in 1779 to make it easier for Paris's wealthy to get to the new Odéon Theatre, which opened the same year – just ten years before the Revolution.

No. 12, rue de l'Odéon, is where a revolution in writing took place. From 1921 to 1940, this was the home of the famous bookshop, **Shakespeare and Company**. It was a home from home for expat writers like Hemingway, Scott Fitzgerald and James Joyce, and the bookshop still operates today but at its new address, 37 rue de la Bûcherie (Métro: Maubert-Mutualité).

ST-GERMAIN-DES-PRÉS

Boulevard St-Germain (1 min)

This street is the main artery of the left bank, running for some 3km (2 miles) from the Pont de Sully in the east to the Pont de la Concorde in the west. In between, it sweeps down through the left bank and Latin Quarter, with the stretch where it crosses the **boulevard St-Michel** (*see* p.69) having as good a claim as any to being the intellectual heart of Paris. Although the street changes direction, it mainly runs in long, straight lines, part of the intention of architect Baron Haussmann, who created the street when redesigning Paris in the late 19th century.

Three well-known cafés are to be found along here, where artists and intellectuals have gathered over the years. At No.170, you will find **Les Deux Magots**, immortalized in Ernest Hemingway's memoir of Paris,

Brasserie Lipp

151 Boulevard St-Germain

Tel: (01) 45 48 53 91

Open: daily 8am–1am

Moderate

Famous for its history, Brasserie Lipp dates from the 19th century and is named after its original owner, one Mr Lippman from Alsace. It is the epitome of Parisian brasseries with an Art Nouveau interior and smartly decked out waiters. The food consists of basic Alsation dishes and Alsation beer.

Café de Flore

A Moveable Feast and again in his novel, *The Sun Also Rises*. Oscar Wilde, Paul Verlaine and Pablo Picasso were also all regulars in their time. Opposite, at No.172 is the art-deco **Café de Flore**, more popular with philosophers and intellecturals of the Left Bank than artists, where in the 1940s, Jean Paul Sartre and Simone de Beauvoir, not only had coffee but practically set up their offices. Albert Camus was another regular. At No.151 you will find **Brasserie Lipp**, long favoured by French leaders, including de Gaulle, Mitterand and Pompidou as well as writers, editors and artists.

Église St-Germain-des-Prés (1 min)

3 place St-Germain-des-Prés
***Tel**: (01) 43 25 41 71*
***Open**: Mon–Sat 8am–7.45pm, Sun 9am–8pm*
***Adm**: free*

A claimant to being the oldest church in Paris (***see** also* St-Julien-le-Pauvre, p.70), this was originally built during the 11th century and rebuilt in 1163, although there has been a church on the site since at least 542. The 11th-century church was greatly restored in the 19th century, but one of the original towers still stands, containing within it one of the oldest belfries in the whole of France. The skull of the French philosopher René Descartes ('I think therefore I am') is buried in the church, and it's worth looking inside to see some of the few original features that remain. A good time to visit is when there is an evening concert of classical music.

Musée National Delacroix (2 mins)

6 rue du Furstemberg
***Tel**: (01) 44 41 86 50; www.musee-delacroix.fr*
***Open**: Wed–Mon 9.30am–5pm*
***Adm**: adults €5, 18–25s €2.60, under-18s free and free on first Sun of each month*

The artist Eugène Delacroix was hired in 1857 to paint some murals at St-Sulpice (***see*** p.74) and moved into this apartment in order to be closer to what would be a lengthy commission. In the event, he stayed here until his death in 1863, and his apartment and studio now form a small museum to his work. Many of his major canvasses can be seen in the Louvre (***see*** p.31) and the Musée d'Orsay (***see*** p.165), but there are enough of his other paintings here to warrant a visit if you're interested. Also on display are his letters, sketches and personal items, including his palette.

ST-SULPICE

Église St-Sulpice (4 mins)

Place St-Sulpice
***Tel**: (01) 46 33 21 78*
***Open**: daily 8am–7pm*
***Adm**: free*

The monumental and rather unusual Classical frontage of this church by Florentine architect Giovanni Servandoni belies the fact that it has a plain but beautifully illuminated interior. Among the highlights are the frescoes by the artist Eugène Delacroix in the *Chapel of the Angels* (***see*** Musée National Delacroix, above), the most famous of these being *Jacob Wrestling with the Angel* and *Heliodorus Driven from the Temple*. The chapel is just to the right of the front door as you enter.

St-Sulpice was founded by the abbey of St-Germain-des-Prés in 1646 and is named after St Sulpicius, a 6th-century archbishop of Bourges, a town to the southwest of Paris. It was intended to be a parish church for the local peasants but they had to wait a long time for it – thanks to a lightning

Église St-Sulpice

Au Vieux Colombier

65 rue de Rennes

Tel: (01) 45 48 53 81

Open: Mon–Sat 8am–midnight, Sun 11am–8pm, food served Mon–Sat noon–10pm, Sun noon–8pm

Inexpensive

Characterful local café where you'll get a slice of real Parisian life along with cheap wine, beer and food. Simple but fun.

strike and cashflow problems, it took 134 years for it to be completed.

The colonnaded façade has two mis-matching towers on each side; the result of changing styles and indecision: in all a total of six different architects were employed during the building period.

In 1776 an organ was designed for the church, using some 6,588 pipes, which makes it one of the largest organs in the world (***see*** Église St-Eustache, p.62). There are regular organ recitals and hearing this instrument in full flow is quite something.

Another feature, rather easier to miss than the organ, is a bronze strip that runs through the north–south transept. This marks the *zero meridian* and it is said to be so perfectly struck by light on three occasions a year that the sunlight shines straight along the strip and reflects up to illuminate a cross directly above it.

The two huge shells inside the front door were given to François I by the Venetian Republic. He had them mounted on sculptures by Jean-Baptiste Pigalle and turned into holy water fonts.

Outside is the place St-Sulpice, which

goes back to 1754, though the central fountain is from 1844 and was designed by Visconti. It's known as the **Fontaine des Quatre Points Cardinaux**, which can mean either the 'Fountain of the Four Cardinal Points' or the 'Fountain of the Four Cardinals Who Never Were'. It's both a visual and verbal pun, as none of the four church figures carved at the four points of the compass ever became Cardinals.

Fontaine des Quatre Points Cardinaux

MONTPARNASSE-BIENVENUE

Tour Montparnasse (2 mins)

33 avenue du Maine
***Tel**: (01) 45 38 52 56*
***Open**: daily 9.30am–10.30pm*
***Adm**: adults €8, concessions €6.80, 5–14s €5.50, under-5s free*

This tower was built in 1973 on the site of the old Montparnasse railway station and, at the time, was Europe's largest office block. It was considered by many to be a real eyesore, a rare high-rise intrusion on the Paris skyline, but today it seems fairly innocuous. At 209m (686ft), it's slightly shorter than the Eiffel Tower (***see** p.87). Take the lift to the 56th floor for a wonderful view, which includes the Eiffel Tower. At the top there is a display of aerial photos of the city, a bar and a restaurant;

Le Ciel de Paris

Tour Montparnasse, 33 avenue du Maine

Tel: (01) 40 64 77 64;

www.cieldeparis.com

Open: daily, lunch and dinner

Expensive

You'll feel on top of the world dining here, up on the 56th floor of the Tour Montparnasse. Or on top of Europe, at the very least, as this stunning setting is the highest restaurant on the continent. It has food to match, and though it's certainly not the cheapest restaurant in Europe, you'll think it worth a visit for that special occasion, gazing out over the Paris skyline.

Tour Montparnasse

Hippopotamus Montparnasse

68 boulevard du Montparnasse

Tel: (01) 40 64 14 97

Open: daily, all day

Moderate

Part of the popular chain of family restaurants, where there are distractions for the children and a wide menu of simple but decent meals.

occasionally there are concerts on the terrace for music lovers who don't suffer from vertigo.

Musée Antoine Bourdelle (4 mins)

16 rue Antoine Bourdelle
***Tel**: (01) 45 48 67 27*
***Open**: Tue–Sun 10am–5.40pm*
***Adm**: free*

Between 1884 and 1929, the sculptor Bourdelle lived and worked here for the last 45 years of his life. A student of Rodin, he was, like the master, a prolific worker. Over 900 pieces are on display including models and plaster casts as well as original works, paintings and drawings. Much of Bourdelle's work was, in fact, for use on public buildings, and thus on a large scale. The best-known are probably the friezes for the Théâtre des Champs-Élysées. He was also commissioned to produce a monument to General Alvear of Argentina, which can be seen in Buenos Aires. Busts of people include Beethoven and Rodin, and the works spill over into the garden.

Jardin de l'Atlantique (2 mins)

Above and behind the Gare Montparnasse
***Open**: daily dawn–dusk*
***Adm**: free*

This garden is one of Montparnasse's hidden secrets, which no visitors ever find by accident. It is behind the Montparnasse railway station, and you reach it down either of the main streets that lead round the back of the station, and then looking for steps leading up above the tracks. The railway tracks are, in fact, some 18m (60ft) below you, with the garden suspended above them; there are a few spots where you can peer down to the tracks below. The garden was opened in 1995 and includes walkways, benches, tennis courts and some meteorological equipment and displays. It's like stumbling on a hidden world in a children's storybook, and despite the fact that it is now over ten years old, few guidebooks even hint at its existence.

Jardin de l'Atlantique

Musée de la Poste (4 mins)

34 boulevard de Vaugirard
***Tel**: (01) 42 79 23 45; www.laposte.fr*
***Open**: Mon–Sat 10am–6pm*
***Adm**: adults €4.50, concessions €3, under-18s free*

Like many museums on specialist subjects – and subjects that might initially seem rather dull – this is absolutely fascinating and full of extraordinary things.

It is run by the French state postal service and tells the engrossing history of the development of postal services throughout the country. Information goes back to 2500 BC and the use of marks on clay tablets. It covers the logistical transportation problems of all sorts of transport: carriages, boats, planes, trains or even pigeons and hot-air balloons – both of which were used to get mail in and out of the city during the Siege of Paris in 1871, with franking marks stamped on the wings of the carrier pigeons.

A separate gallery deals with the evolution and design of more conventional postage stamps, and you don't need to be a philatelist to appreciate the beauty, variety and ingenuity that has gone into them over the years.

La Coupole (1 min)

102 boulevard du Montparnasse
***Tel**: (01) 43 20 14 20*
***Open**: daily 7am–2am*

Paris probably has almost as many well-known eating and drinking establishments as it does conventional tourist sites. The Coupole first opened its doors in 1927 and very quickly became one of the city's most fashionable dining and dancing establishments, despite being a little to the south of the centre. People made their way here from all walks of life, drawn by the Art Deco décor and the pillars decorated by many of the famous artists who frequented the place, such as Brancusi and Chagall. Man Ray dined here, too as did Picasso, Hemingway, Sartre and, more recently, the film director Roman Polanski. La Coupole serves typical brasserie fare at a reasonable price, but in fantastic surroundings.

Musée Zadkine (6 mins)

100 bis rue d'Assas
***Tel**: (01) 55 42 77 20;*
www.paris.fr/musees/zadkine
***Open**: Tue–Sun 10am–6pm*
***Adm**: free, charge for exhibitions*

The Russian-born sculptor Ossip Zadkine made his home in Paris and in particular in this little house near the Luxembourg Gardens, where he lived for almost 40 years till his death in 1967. He was one of the original Cubists but his later work ranged more widely, covering themes such as religion and mythology, and encompassing other styles such as Abstractionism and Expressionism. Two of his best-known works are monuments to Vincent Van Gogh, one in Holland and one in Auvers-sur-Oise, where Van Gogh died. Here there are several busts and portraits of Van Gogh, and a plaster cast of the Auvers statue.

Rue Campagne-Première

RASPAIL

Rue Campagne-Première (1 min)

This street right by the Métro and the Montparnasse Cemetery will be of interest to lovers of art and architecture alike. It has several attractive Art Deco buildings, and has been home to many artists over the years, including Modigliani at no. 3, Picasso, Kandinsky and Joan Miró.

DENFERT-ROCHEREAU

The Catacombs (1 min)

1 place Denfert Rochereau
***Tel**: (01) 43 22 47 63*
***Open**: Tue–Sun 10am–6pm*
***Adm**: adults €5, over-60s €3.30, students and 14–26s €2.50, under-14s free*

Many of Paris's best attractions are under the ground, like the Métro, of course, the Sewers (***see*** p.129), the crypts of the Panthéon (***see*** p.138) and these, the Catacombs. This vast collection of human

Contre-Allée

83 avenue Denfert-Rochereau

Tel: (01) 43 54 99 86; www.contreallee.com

Open: Sun–Fri lunch and dinner, Sat dinner

Moderate

Terrific bistro serving superior food at affordable prices, with a terrace in summer and, rare for Paris, a non-smoking room.

bones owes its existence to the fact that there used to be several quarries in this part of Paris. These underground tunnel networks have existed since Roman times.

When the city's cemeteries were running out of space towards the end of the 18th century it was decided to make use of the quarries and tunnels to dispose of the dead. The tunnels were used as bone depositories for almost a hundred years, and as a result it is said that the remains of an estimated six million Parisians are stored here – and that's a lot of bones.

The bones are now stacked high, and you walk along corridors between walls of tightly packed thigh bones, beyond which are more bones, and occasionally mounds of neatly stacked skulls. It's a chilling indeed a chilly experience, as it can be quite cold below ground, and children tend to love it. During World War II, when the Nazis occupied the city, the French Resistance used the tunnels as secret meeting places.

Observatoire de Paris (3 mins)

61 avenue de l'Observatoire
Tel*: (01) 40 51 22 21*
Open*: 1st Sat each month at 2.30, but must be booked in advance by post*

Just a short walk from the Catacombs is the Paris Observatory, neatly situated on what, until 1884,was the city's zero degrees longitude.

The construction of the observatory itself began propitiously on the summer solstice, 21 June 1667, and was finished five years later. The observatory immediately allowed scientists to calculate the dimensions of the solar system, to calculate the speed of light and to draw a detailed map of the moon. All this within less than ten years of the opening. There is a small museum here and it's possible to visit the museum and the observatory, but it is quite a procedure, and you have to prove your credentials. If you are genuinely interested then ring the observatory to set things in motion.

The Eiffel Tower

LINE 6

CHARLES DE GAULLE ÉTOILE – NATION

The second line to be opened in Paris was a section of Line 6 just three stations from the Arc de Triomphe to the Trocadéro on 2 October 1900. Line 6 takes visitors to the several attractions around the Trocadéro, and on to the Eiffel Tower on the south side if the river. Then it swings through the southern part of Paris, linking with Montparnasse station and around back up and across the river to its eastern terminus at Nation. A ride on Line 6 is unusual in that much more of it is above ground and you get a good look at the Paris streets.

CHARLES DE GAULE ÉTOILE

Arc de Triomphe, *see* p.74

KLÉBER

BOISSIÈRE

TROCADÉRO

Palais de Chaillot 84

Cité de l'Architecture et du Patrimoine 85

Musée de l'Homme 85

Musée de la Marine 86

Jardins du Trocadéro 86

PASSY

BIR-HAKEIM (CHAMP DE MARS TOUR EIFFEL)

Eiffel Tower 87

DUPLEIX

LA MOTTE-PICQUET-GRENELLE

CAMBRONNE

SÈVRES-LECOURBE

PASTEUR

MONTPARNASSE–BIENVENUE

Tour Montparnasse, *see* p.76

Musée Antoine 77
Bourdelle, *see* p.77

Jardin de l'Atlantique, *see* p.77

Musée de la Poste, *see* p.78

EDGAR-QUINET

Cimetière du Montparnasse 90

RASPAIL

Rue Campagne-Première, *see* p.80

DENFERT–ROCHEREAU

The Catacombs, *see* p.80

Observatoire de Paris, *see* p.81

CHARLES DE GAULE ÉTOILE

***See* Line 1, p.14**
Arc de Triomphe p.14

TROCADÉRO

Palais de Chaillot (1 min)

Place du Trocadéro

A favourite viewing spot for the Eiffel Tower, and indeed a recommended place for your first view of it, is from the Trocadéro Gardens behind the huge 1930s' Palais de Chaillot, which is impossible to miss as you emerge from the Métro onto the place du Trocadéro. Napoleon had his eye on this little hill and meant to build a palace here for his son, but his empire came tumbling down and it never happened. A palace was built here in 1878 for the Universal Exhibition, but that was replaced by the present building in 1937, also put up for an exhibition. It now houses several museums (***see*** below) and a theatre, and behind is a splendid view of the Eiffel Tower. You can walk to the tower from here, down through the gardens and across the river.

Le Butte Chaillot

110bis avenue Kléber

Tel: (01) 47 27 88 88

Open: Sun–Fri lunch and dinner, Sat dinner

Expensive

Arty bistro run by superchef Guy Savoy, with superior dishes at an affordable price. For less formal options there are numerous little cafés around the place du Trocadéro.

Palais de Chaillot

Le Totem

17 place du Trocadéro

Tel: (01) 47 27 28 29; www.letotem.fr

Open: Tue–Sat lunch and dinner

Moderate

Taking its name from the totems on display in the Musée de l'Homme next door, this is the perfect place to pause for lunch or a drink – there's a bar as well as indoor and outdoor dining. The food is first class, as is the view of the Eiffel Tower across the river.

Cité de l'Architecture et du Patrimoine (1 min)

***Open**: due to open in 2005*

In 1997 a fire gutted the eastern wing of the Palais and the two museums it contained were closed. The **Cinema Museum** has been moved further out of the city to Bercy in the east, and will reopen in 2005. The other, the Museum of French Monuments, will return to the Palais but with additions and under a grand new name, the **City of Architecture and Patrimony**. It will tell the story of French architecture from the Middle Ages onwards.

Musée de l'Homme (1 min)

Palais de Chaillot, place du Trocadéro

***Tel**: (01) 44 05 72 72; www.mnhn.fr*

***Open**: Wed–Mon 9.45am–5.15pm*

***Adm**: adults €5, over-60s, students under-27 and 4–16s €3, under-4s free*

Despite its rather old-fashioned setting, this Museum of Mankind is a fascinating collection that should appeal to everyone from young children upwards. The children will probably respond to the displays on tattooing, head-shrinking and how the Egyptians made a mummy, while adults might be more impressed by the excellent collection of over 400 musical instruments, the displays on native American culture, the Easter Island statue or the re-creation of a Mayan Temple from Central America.

The museum spans the whole world, and there are items dating back to 3.5 million years BC – the sections on early man and evolution are especially good, showing how tools developed and giving a feeling of what it was like to live in prehistoric times.

However, displays also deal with contemporary issues, with interactive computer displays and exhibitions on thought-provoking subjects such as genetics, AIDS and population growth. Note that some of the displays are being transferred for use in a new ethnology museum, due to open late 2005. Paris museums are in a

Musée de l'Homme

state of change in 2005, with many refurbishments and imminent openings and closings, so be prepared for anything.

Musée de la Marine (1 min)

Palais de Chaillot, place du Trocadéro
***Tel:** (01) 53 65 69 69; www.musee-marine.fr*
***Open**: Wed–Mon 10am–6pm*
***Adm**: adults €6, over-60s and 19–25s €4, 6–18s €3, under-6s free*

Worth a visit for anyone interested in ships, the museum covers French naval history, right back to the earliest days, and includes some fascinating scale models of ships in incredible detail. There are also naval paintings, uniforms, maps, books and navigation equipment ancient and modern, odd bits of boats and ever-intriguing examples of ships in bottles.

Jardins du Trocadéro (1 min)

Palais de Chaillot, place du Trocadéro
***Open**: 24 hours*

Immediately behind the Palais de Chaillot is a terrace from where there's a picture-postcard view of the Eiffel Tower. From the terrace, steps lead down to the Trocadéro Gardens, which were created at the same time as the Palais for the 1937 Exhibition. There's a long pool leading down towards

Jardins du Trocadéro

the river and directly in line with the Eiffel Tower. There are also statues and a fountain, and shady tree-lined paths. It's lovely at any time but is a particularly good place to go at night, when the tower is lit up and the fountains are floodlit.

Altitude 95
1st Level, Eiffel Tower
Tel: (01) 45 55 20 04
Open: daily, lunch and dinner
Moderate
Excellent location for its Paris views, and you can also dine here and bypass the queues for the tower itself. It isn't cheap, but there are lunchtime *prix fixe* menus that keep the cost down, and the suitably metallic décor is great fun.

BIR-HAKEIM (CHAMP DE MARS TOUR EIFFEL)

Eiffel Tower (7 mins)

Champ de Mars
***Tel**: (01) 44 11 23 45, or (01) 44 11 23 23 for recorded information; www.tour-eiffel.fr*
***Open**: daily 9.30am–11pm (9am–midnight Jun–Aug)*
***Adm**: from €3.30–10.20 depending on when, how far and how you ascend. Reductions for 3–12s and under-3s free.*

It is hard now to imagine the Paris skyline without the Eiffel Tower, but the structure was much criticized when it first went up in 1889 for the Universal Exhibition. At the time it was the tallest building in the world at 320m (1050ft) and remained so until the arrival of the Empire State Building in 1931. You will see the tower frequently as you move around Paris and no first visit to the city is complete without ascending it.

Going up the tower requires a little thought and a little planning. Queues are usually very long and it is worth getting there before it opens to minimize the wait. Queues tend to be shorter at night, and an evening ascent when the tower is floodlit is atmospheric. You should also decide in advance whether you want to go all the way to the top, and plan how to get there.

If you want to go to the top on the third level, you have to change lifts at the second level. You can also reach the second level (but no further) by climbing the stairs, but it is a long climb from the first to the second level. Another way to beat the queues is to climb the stairs to the first level and take the lift there as the people coming up get out.

To get to the first level there are 360 steps, taking you to 57m (187ft). The restaurant, Altitude 95, is here and you can jump the queue for the lifts by booking a table here and going straight up. There's also a small museum with audiovisual displays, and a post office on this level – if you send cards from here they will have an Eiffel Tower postmark. It's another 700 steps up to the second level.

But the top is what everyone aims for and the views are rewarding. It's said that you can see for up to 80kms (50 miles) on a good day, and even on a poor day the views of the city are second to none. Up here there is a display area, and the architect Gustave Eiffel's sitting room; once the tower was built he kept an office up at the top, using it for experiments until his death in 1923.

Eiffel had made his name building bridges and viaducts, and was a master of using wrought-iron to create graceful designs. The facts and figures about the tower are fascinating. You might even say riveting. The tower has 2.5 million rivets, holding together 18,000 metal parts. On hot days these expand by up to 15cm (6 inches), while on the windiest days the tower sways by no more than 12cm (4.5 inches), thanks to its solid construction and its immense weight – 10,100 metric tons.

Jules Verne

2nd Level, Eiffel Tower

Tel: (01) 45 55 61 44

Open: daily, lunch and dinner

Walking time: 7 mins

Expensive

More *haute cuisine* than the Altitude 95 a level below, and even better views of the Paris skyline. Expect to pay handsomely for the gourmet food, but it's worth it if you book ahead and can get a table in what must be one of the most romantic dining places in the world.

Eiffel Tower

There were those who wanted to see the tower torn down as soon as it went up, and the writer Guy de Maupassant allegedly said how much he enjoyed having lunch at the Eiffel Tower because it was the only place that he didn't have to look at it.

MONTPARNASSE-BIENVENUE

See Line 4, p.76

Tour Montparnasse p.76, Musée Antoine Bourdelle p.77, Jardin de l'Atlantique p.77, Musée de la Poste p.78

EDGAR-QUINET

Cimetière du Montparnasse (1 min)

3 boulevard Edgar-Quinet
***Tel**: (01) 44 10 86 50*
***Open**: Mar–Oct Mon–Fri 8am–6pm, Sat 8.30am–6pm, Sun 9am–6pm; Nov–Feb Mon–Fri 8am–5.30pm, Sat 8.30am–5.30pm, Sun 9.30am–5.30pm*
***Adm**: free*

Père-Lachaise (**see** p.58) may have more famous names, but this smaller cemetery is also worth a pilgrimage, especially for literature lovers. Several great writers are buried here, including the Irish writer and long-time Paris resident, Samuel Beckett. Beckett, who wrote *Waiting for Godot* and won the Nobel Prize for Literature, first studied in Paris and then came here to live in 1937. He found the city a congenial home where he could have the anonymity he sought. He died here in 1989.

The French writer famous for his brilliant short stories, Guy de Maupassant, is also here. His grave is notable for the open book carving on the top of it. Buried here too is the poet Charles Baudelaire, who shocked the world with his frank collection of poems, *Les Fleurs du Mal* (*Flowers of Evil*). Close to the main gates you can find the joint grave of the philosopher-writers Jean-Paul Sartre and Simone de Beauvoir, together in death and inseparable companions in life although they never lived together.

It isn't only the graves of writers that make the cemetery stand out. Allow an hour or so to wander round, as the cemetery is small enough to find almost everything if you look. There is an office near the entrance where you can get a map of the most-visited graves and attendants are happy to direct you to others if they are not already marked.

One grave that is absolutely charming is that of Charles Pigeon and his family. Who was Charles Pigeon? He invented the gas lamp and his grave shows him sitting up in bed with his wife reading by lamp light. Another notable grave decoration is one called *The Kiss*, a beautifully simple sculpture by the artist Brancusi, which marks his own final resting place.

Others buried here include the composer Saint-Saëns and the sculptor Zadkine, whose museum and studio are only a short walk away (**see** p.79). A less well-known sculptor buried here is Frédéric Bartholdi, although the whole world knows his work as he built the Statue of Liberty for New York.

Café de la Place

23 rue d'Odessa

Tel: (01) 42 18 01 55

Open: daily, all day, food served Mon–Sat noon–1am, Sun noon–10pm

Inexpensive

Ideal Parisian café, with pavement seating in summer and a basic but decent menu and always busy with local people.

The photographer Man Ray is here, and so too is the singer Serge Gainsbourg, the actress Jean Seberg and the absurdist playwright, Ionesco. If you see the name André Citroën on a grave then, yes, it belongs to the well-known car manufacturer.

Montparnasse Cemetery was opened in 1824, on land that had previously been three farms – you can still see the remains of a 17th-century windmill in one corner. It was quite an occasion when it opened as no new cemetery had been built in Paris since 1786, when the city authorities banned new cemeteries too close to the city. This was because of an incident at another cemetery, the Cimetière des Innocents, where overcrowding was causing graves to open and bodies to rise to the surface. Banning cemeteries altogether naturally did little to help the overcrowding problem, and eventually a new place had to be found. It was at Montparnasse.

RASPAIL

***See* Line 4, p.80**

Rue Campagne-Première, p.80

DENFERT-ROCHEREAU

***See* Line 4, p.80**

The Catacombs p.80, Observatoire de Paris p.81

Val-de-Grâce

LINE 7

LA CORNEUVE 8 MAI 1945 TO VILLEJUIF – LOUIS ARAGON OR MARIE D'IVRY

Line 7 is the longest Métro line in Paris, snaking for 22.4km (14 miles) from the far southeast of the city through the centre and out to the further northwest suburbs, running underground the whole way. The first section was opened in 1910; it was changed and added to piecemeal over the years, With the final extension added in 1987. The first section to be opened – from Porte d'Orléans to Porte de la Villette to the northeast of the city centre – was the first true branch of the Métro, taking the trains out of the city centre loop for the first time. During rush hour, this line has the most trains because of its length.

PALAIS ROYAL MUSÉE DU LOUVRE

Comédie Française, ***see*** p.26

Palais Royal, ***see*** p.27

Place des Victoires, ***see*** p.28

Arc de Triomphe du Carrousel, ***see*** p.29

Musée des Arts Décoratifs, ***see*** p.29

Musée de la Mode et du Textile, ***see*** p.29

Musée de la Publicité, ***see*** p.29

PONT NEUF

Pont Neuf 94

Paris Plage 95

Square du Vert-Galant 95

Place Dauphine 96

CHÂTELET

PONT MARIE

Hôtel de Sens 96

Île St-Louis 97

Église St-Louis-en-l'Île 98

Hôtel de Lauzun 98

Maison Européenne de la Photographie 99

Musée de la Curiosité et de la Magie 99

SULLY-MORLAND

JUSSIEU

Arènes de Lutèce, ***see*** p.140

Jardin des Plantes, ***see*** p.141

Natural History Museum, ***see*** p.142

Paris Zoo *(La Ménagerie)*, ***see*** p.143

PLACE MONGE

Rue Mouffetard 100

Place de la Contrescarpe 101

CENSIER-DAUBENTON

St-Médard 102

Val-de-Grâce 103

Mosquée de Paris 104

OPÉRA

Opéra National de Paris Garnier, ***see*** p.115

Musée de l'Opéra, ***see*** p.116

Musée de la Parfumerie Fragonard, ***see*** p.117

Musée de la Parfumerie Fragonard (second branch), ***see*** p.118

PYRAMIDES

OPÉRA

See Line 8, p.115

Opéra National de Paris Garnier p.115, Musée de l'Opéra p.116, Musée de la Parfumerie Fragonard p.117, Musée de la Parfumerie Fragonard (second branch) p.118

PALAIS ROYAL MUSÉE DU LOUVRE

See Line 1, p.26

Comédie Française p.26, Palais Royal p.27, Place des Victoires p.28, Arc de Triomphe du Carrousel p.29, Musée des Arts Décoratifs p.29, Musée de la Mode et du Textile p.29, Musée de la Publicité p.29

PONT NEUF

Pont Neuf (1 min)

Pont Neuf, or the New Bridge is, naturally, the oldest bridge in Paris. It dates back to 1578, and took 30 years to build. At the west end of the Île de la Cité, it's a lovely bridge to walk across, with good river views, especially at night when the lights come on. It leads to an attractive area of the island, at its western end, where there is a statue of Henri IV (who built the bridge) and all around are bars, hotels, restaurants and squares called Henri IV. The first statue was put up in 1635 but was destroyed during the French Revolution. The current one is a

Taverne Henri IV

13 place du Pont-Neuf

Tel: (01) 43 54 27 90

Open: Mon–Fri lunch and dinner, Sat lunch

Moderate

Long-standing old-fashioned wine–bistro, serving excellent food at very reasonable prices – which is why it's usually packed.

Pont Neuf

Paris Plage

replacement from 1818. This was the first bridge in Paris not to have houses built on it, and also the first that had pavements reserved for pedestrians. It has remained a favourite bridge for Parisians ever since.

Paris Plage (2 mins)

Right bank from Pont Neuf to Pont de Sully
***Open**: Mid-Jul–mid-Aug, daily 9.30am–11pm*
***Adm**: free*

Paris Plage, initiated in July–August 2002, is Paris's answer to the beach, offering white sand, palm trees, sun loungers, a couple of swimming pools, ice cream sellers and beach games along two miles of the right bank of the Seine, from the Pont Neuf to the Pont de Sully. It was very popular from the start and has become an annual event, with themed years (Brazil in 2005, complete with capoeira classes in front of the Hôtel de Ville) and free sporting activities, including dancing, pétanque and volleyball, as well as open-air concerts. One thing, a beach it may be but the Seine is still not fit to swim in.

Square du Vert-Galant (2 mins)

From the statue of Henri IV on the Pont Neuf, steps lead down to this hidden little square, which roughly translates as the Square of the Gallant Green Man. A 'green' gentleman was one who was known to be lusty, and this refers to Henri IV who was renowned for his love of the ladies. It's a shady place, which makes you feel very close to the river, almost on the prow of a boat, and if you want to set sail you can do it from here, as it's one of the places where the river cruise boats pull up.

Yugaraj

14 rue Dauphine

Tel: (01) 43 26 44 91; www.yugaraj.com

Open: Tue–Wed and Fri–Sun lunch and dinner, Thu dinner

Moderate

Sometimes Paris's non-French restaurants get overlooked, so crowded is the city with first-class food from all over the country, yet this stylish Indian restaurant stands out. It focuses on modern-style cooking with a subtle use of spices, way beyond the usual high street standards, and is naturally more expensive.

Place Dauphine

Place Dauphine (3 mins)

The statue of Henri IV marks another hidden gem – directly opposite and across the bridge is the entrance to the delightful place Dauphine. The 'Dauphin' was Henri IV's son, (later Louis XIII), and the square was planned by Henri IV in 1607 as one of his first projects when making plans for the improvement of the city. Today it contains a few shops, eating places and a hotel, as well as many fine old town houses, with no. 14 being one of the best unrestored properties.

CHÂTELET

See Line 4, Les Halles p.62

Les Halles p.62, Église St-Eustache p.62

PONT MARIE

Hôtel de Sens (1 min)

1 rue Figuier
***Tel**: (01) 42 78 14 60*
***Open**: Tue–Fri 1.30–8.15pm, Sat 10am–8.15pm*
***Adm**: adults €4, concessions €2, under-12s free*

The Hôtel de Sens is the oldest surviving mansion in the Marais, dating from the 15th century, just behind the Quai des Celestins on the right bank. It was built between 1475 and 1507 as a Parisian home for the archbishops of Sens, and later was

Hôtel de Sens

L'Enoteca
25 rue Charles V
Tel: (01) 42 78 91 44
Open: daily, lunch and dinner
Moderate
Lively Italian wine bar with a good menu and plenty of Italian wines by the glass, if you're ready for a brief change from French food.

the headquarters for the Lyons Stage Coach Company. The journey from Paris to Lyons, France's second city in the south, was so fraught with danger that passengers used to write their wills before making it. In the turrets of the Hôtel is the **Bibliothèque Forney**, a library dedicated to the applied and graphic arts. It is possible to visit the mansion, which sometimes puts on graphic art exhibitions.

Île St-Louis (1 min)

In the opposite direction, across the Pont Marie is the Île St-Louis. It has become a cliché to describe cities like London and New York as collections of villages, but on this, smaller of Paris's two islands in the middle of the River Seine you really could feel as if you were in a little French village. That's apart from the fact that it was built on a grid, although it only has one main street. It's been a popular and exclusive city address since the 17th century, when many

of its mansions were built. A few of these are now hotels, and they are marvellous places to stay.

Île St-Louis

Église St-Louis-en-l'Île (4 mins)

19bis rue St-Louis-en-l'Île
Tel: *(01) 46 34 11 60*
Open: *Tue–Sun 9am–noon and 3–7pm*
Adm: *free*

This delightful Baroque church was completed in 1726, after 62 years of work. It was designed by the royal architect, Louis Le Vau, who lived on the island and who was also responsible for parts of Versailles and the Louvre. Because of its location on the charming and exclusive Île St-Louis, it is in great demand for weddings, and concerts are also popular here. Inside is a statue of St Louis, after whom the church and the island are named, as is the American city in Missouri, as a plaque in the church makes clear.

Église St-Louis-en-l'Île

Hôtel de Lauzun (4 mins)

17 quai d'Anjou
Tel: *(01) 44 61 20 00*
Open: *not open to the general public*

This Hôtel was also built by Louis Le Vau (***see*** above) in 1656, but the person for whom it was designed, a corrupt Army caterer, was arrested not long afterwards and so the building is named for its second owner, the Duke of Lauzun. It's notorious for being the meeting place of the '*hashish club*' organized by the poet Baudelaire in

La Tour d'Argent

15–17 quai de la Tournelle

Tel: (01) 43 54 23 31; www.latourdargent.com

Open: Wed–Sun lunch and dinner, Tue dinner

Expensive

Easily one of the best restaurants in the city for food, service and location – try and get a window table, overlooking the river and Notre-Dame. It dates back to 1582 and the simple but superb duck à l'orange is its signature dish. It has one of the best cellars in the world, and the sommelier is an Englishman!

1834, which the author Balzac and the painter Manet attended. Other visitors to the Hôtel – not necessarily for the hashish club – have included Delacroix, Wagner and Rilke. The interior remains as it was when it was originally built, but unfortunately, it isn't open to the public.

Maison Européenne de la Photographie (2 mins)

5–7 rue de Fourcy
***Tel**: (01) 44 78 75 00; www.mep-fr.org*
***Open**: Wed–Sun 11am–7.30pm*
***Adm**: adults €5, students and over-60s €2.50, under-8s free and free on Wed 5–8pm*

Slightly north of the Métro, this excellent photography gallery puts on constantly changing displays by some of the world's best photographers, with several on show at any one time in its various small but well-lit galleries. Moving as well as still photography gets a look-in, and there are also displays from the gallery's own permanent collection. The Maison's broad remit also covers the best of reportage and portrait photography. In addition, it acts as a meeting place for students and photographers, with a library and archive, and there is a very good and stylish little café and a rather cramped bookshop.

Musée de la Curiosité et de la Magie (3 mins)

11 rue St-Paul
***Tel**: (01) 42 72 13 26; www.museedelamagie.com*
***Open**: Wed, Sat, Sun 2–7pm (variable longer hours during school holidays)*
***Adm**: adults €7, 3–12s €5, under-3s free*

This is another of Paris's little gems, a collection of magic props and tricks on display in several basement rooms. There are plenty of fun things to do, like looking in the distorting mirrors and seeing if you can discover how some of the visual illusions are created. There are also regular magic displays, usually in French but the performers will adapt to other languages depending on the numbers. A trick is a trick, though, and doesn't always need words to be appreciated. There's a shop for those who want to buy a few magic tricks, although parts of it are for professionals only and sealed off from the general public.

Mémorial de la Shoah, *see* St-Paul, p.39

JUSSIEU

See Line 10, p.140

Arènes de Lutèce p.140, Jardin des Plantes p.141, Natural History Museum p.142, Paris Zoo *(La Ménagerie)* p.143

PLACE MONGE

Rue Mouffetard (2 mins)

The rue Mouffetard features frequently in literature about Paris, and in particular visitors should read Ernest Hemingway's book, *A Moveable Feast*, one of the best books about Paris, in which the street is well described. There's a lot to say about it because it has existed for a long time.

As a street it's been around since the 13th century, but long before that it marked the main Roman road leading southeast out of Paris towards the second city, Lyons, and onward to Rome itself. The hill that the modern street descends was known in Roman times as Mont Cétar, from which it's thought the name 'Mouffetard' derives.

Rue Mouffetard

Le Verre à Pied

118bis rue Mouffetard

Tel: (01) 43 31 15 72

Open: Tue–Sat 9am–9pm, Sun 9am–3pm, food served Tue–Sun noon–2.30pm

Inexpensive

This is a real Paris neighbourhood café, popular with workers from the rue Mouffetard market, and with other locals and visitors too. You can have a coffee, glass of wine or a full lunch (no food in the evenings), and see if you remember seeing it in the film *Amélie*.

Café Delmas

2–4 place de la Contrescarpe

Tel: (01) 43 26 51 26

Open: daily, 8am–2am (Fri–Sat 4am), food served daily 11.30am–11.30pm

Inexpensive

This is Hemingway territory, and the Delmas manages to combine modern style with the old atmosphere of this characterful neighbourhood, where chic meets cheap. The food is simple but good, though most people just want to sit and chat and watch the world over a cup of coffee or a glass of wine.

As you walk along the street, look up when you can (not always easy as there's a regular and very lively market here) to see the lovely, old 17th-century houses that still stand, some of them with unusual decorations and with their original Mansard roofs. Ones to watch out for include no. 12 for the painting above the shop, no. 125 with a restored façade, and no. 134 for its general painted decoration.

Down below, there are now several cafés and food shops, and the daily market, which is one of the best in Paris. It's not the biggest, but the variety of produce is incredible, ranging from everyday household food purchases to gourmet delights. It runs all day, every day, except for Sunday afternoons, and spills over into some of the side streets, so be sure to search out every corner. There are also plenty of good and atmospheric eating places in and around the rue Mouffetard, which are especially busy on Sunday lunchtime when the market has closed.

Place de la Contrescarpe (2 mins)

This pretty and ancient old square also features in Hemingway's Parisian sketches, *A Moveable Feast*. It has smartened up a little since then, and is well established on the tourist trail, but is still recognizable as the rather seedy place that the American author describes. He was quite at home here, being at the time a poverty-stricken writer just trying to make a living as best he could, like many of those around him

Like the rue Mouffetard, this square has a long and colourful past, being a notoriously dangerous place in the Middle Ages. It was then outside the city walls, on the far side of the protective moat on the counter-escarpment, the *contrescarpe*. Part of that old city wall is visible today, although the square as we see it now was laid out in 1852.

Hemingway ate, drank and wrote at a café called **La Chope**, which is still there today between the place and the adjoining rue Lacépède. At no. 1 on the place itself was the

Place de la Contrescarpe

Maison de la Pomme de Pin, a 16th-century café where the writer Rabelais and the rest of the day's literati would hang out. The name can still be seen on a plaque on the wall above the modern-day shop, the Pine Cone Club. Rabelais wrote *Pantagruel* (1532) and *Gargantua* (1534) and caused the word 'Rabelaisian' to be coined, meaning 'expressing humanist values in terms of satirical and earthy humour'. The square is still a popular place for hanging out in, especially with the students from the nearby university. You'll always find it busy in the evenings and on the weekends, although during the day it tends to be slightly quieter and have the air of a French town square with its cafés and bars, and locals going to and from the nearby market.

CENSIER-DAUBENTON

St-Médard (1 min)

141 rue Mouffetard
***Tel**: (01) 44 08 87 00*
***Open**: Tue–Sat 8am–12.30pm and 2.30–7pm, Sun 4–7pm*
***Adm**: free*

At the bottom end of the rue Mouffetard stands this lovely church, which dates back to the 9th century. In those days it was a rural country chapel, standing beside the River Bièvre, which is still here but flows underground. The church is named after St Médard, who handed out wreaths of white roses to young girls who were known to have been especially virtuous. Given the area's later reputation for danger and debauchery, he wouldn't have been buying too many white roses from the flower stalls of the rue Mouffetard market.

Although the site of this church goes back to the 9th century when the chapel was constructed, the present building dates to the middle of the 15th century, which is when work on it began. However, it wasn't finished until 1655 and was renovated in 1773.

The church is noted for several things, including being identified in Victor Hugo's *Les Misérables* as the church where the central character Jean Valjean accidentally meets Javert. A group known as the Convulsionaries used to meet in the garden, when it was a churchyard, drawn to the grave of a young church deacon, François Paris, who died in 1727 and who was said to be responsible for miracle cures.

Val-de-Grâce (10 mins)

Place Alphonse-Laveran
***Tel**: (01) 40 51 47 28*
***Open**: Tue–Wed and Sat–Sun noon–6pm*
***Adm**: adults €4.60, 6–12s €2.30, under-6s free*

This magnificent Baroque church is slightly out of the way but well worth the short journey to get there. It has a charming origin and goes back to 1645, when a seven-year-old Louis XIV laid the foundation stone. The church was built by his mother, Anne of Austria, wife of Louis XIII, to give thanks for the safe birth of the young Louis. She had vowed to erect a magnificent temple if God would only bless her with a son, and Louis was the first of two. The church was certainly a magnificent temple, and is especially noted for its dome and a fresco in the cupola by Pierre Mignard, which features more than 200 figures that are three times life size. Given that Louis XIV went on to reign flamboyantly as the Sun King it seems highly appropriate that

Val-de-Grâce

the church built to honour his birth should itself be so flamboyant with larger-than-life elements. Adjoining the church is a former Benedictine convent, which became a military teaching hospital after the Revolution, and remains a hospital to this day.

Mosquée de Paris (5 mins)

1 place du Puits-de-l'Ermite
***Tel**: (01) 45 35 97 33; www.mosquee-de-paris.com*
***Open**: guided tours only, Sat–Thu 9am–noon and 2–6pm, closed Fri and Muslim holidays*
***Adm**: adults €2.30, over-60s and 7–25s €1.50, under-7s free*

France has always had very close ties with North African countries such as Algeria, Egypt and Tunisia, and has a sizeable Muslim population, mostly Algerian. Many of them live in this quarter, hence the number of ethnic restaurants and, of course, the presence of the mosque. It was

L'Equitable

1 rue des Fossés-St-Marcel

Tel: (01) 43 31 69 20

Open: Tue–Sat lunch and dinner

Inexpensive

First rate bistro with old stone walls and an emphasis on food not decoration, with the lunchtime fixed-price menu of €20.50 being one of the best bargains in the neighbourhood. Definitely a place to head for if you want good food on a budget.

Mosquée de Paris

built in the 1920s, which shows how long the local Muslims have been here.

As well as being a place of prayer, the mosque is also a cultural centre, meeting place and tourist attraction. Visitors can enjoy the tea room and the Turkish baths, and buy a bird cage or a souvenir in the gift shop. There's also a sunken garden to admire, too, but visitors must never forget that this is primarily a place of worship and non-Muslims are requested not to enter the prayer rooms at any time. The mosque is closed on the main holy day, Friday, as well as on Muslim holidays. It's an unusual and attractive building to find in Paris, with a 33m- (108ft) high minaret and tiled courtyards, and a grand patio inspired by Spain's Alhambra Palace. The tea room is especially relaxing, whether you sip a mint tea or tuck into a bowl of couscous.

Opera Garnier

LINE 8

BALARD – CRÉTEIL-PRÉFECTURE

The first section of Line 8 goes back to July 1913 when it was linked to Opéra station, an increasingly busy hub on the network, and ran out southwest as far as the station at Beaugrenelle, now called Charles Michels, on Line 10. The line has been re-routed and extended over the years, and one unusual feature is that the open-air section at the far southeast end of the line as it goes to Créteil runs down the middle of a motorway. Few visitors will have any reason to travel out that far, but you might see a lot of the line in the centre of Paris as a journey on Line 8 will take you to several big attractions, including Napoleon's Tomb and the Invalides, the place de la Madeleine and the Rodin Museum.

ÉCOLE MILITAIRE

Rue Cler 108

LA TOUR MAUBOURG

Hôtel des Invalides 108

Musée de l'Armée 109

Dôme Church and Napoleon's Tomb 110

Musée National Rodin 110

INVALIDES

CONCORDE

Place de la Concorde, *see* p.22

Jeu de Paume, *see* p.23

Musée de L'Orangerie *see* p.24

MADELEINE

Place de la Madeleine 112

Église de la Madeleine 113

Rue du Faubourg-St-Honoré 114

OPÉRA

Opéra National de Paris Garnier 115

Musée de l'Opéra 116

Musée de la Parfumerie Fragonard 117

Musée de la Parfumerie Fragonard (second branch) 118

RICHELIEU-DROUOT

GRANDS BOULEVARDS

Musée Grévin 118

Les Passages 119

BONNE NOUVELLE

STRASBOURG ST-DENIS

RÉPUBLIQUE

FILLES DU CALVAIRE

Cirque d'Hiver Bouglione 120

ST-SÉBASTIEN-FROISSART

CHEMIN VERT

BASTILLE

L'Opéra, *see* p.40

Canal St-Martin, *see* p.41

Richard Lenoir Market, *see* p.42

Rue de Lappe, *see* p.42

Rue du Faubourg-St-Antoine, *see* p.42

Promenade Plantée, *see* p.43

Viaduc des Arts, *see* p.44

Place des Vosges, *see* p.44

Maison de Victor Hugo, *see* p.45

LEDRU-ROLLIN

Aligre Market 121

Rue Cler market

ÉCOLE MILITAIRE

Rue Cler (1 min)

Rue Cler is one of Paris's best-known market streets, patronized by the well-heeled local residents who include several politicians and foreign diplomats. The main street is pedestrianized for the market (Tue–Sat, all day), and many of the other streets around here are full of chic little shops, smart cafés and restaurants, and several stylish boutique hotels. One shop specializes in Breton food and drink, there are wine merchants, patisseries, butchers, bakers, greengrocers and several specialist cheese shops – just follow your nose. Don't forget your eyes, either, and take a look at nos. 33 and 151 in particular, which have Art Nouveau designs.

Le Café du Marché

38 rue Cler

Tel: (01) 47 05 51 27

Open: Mon–Sat 7am–midnight, Sun 7am–5pm, food served Mon–Sat 11.30am–11pm, Sun 11.30am–3.30pm

Inexpensive

The food is excellent yet inexpensive and the atmosphere is terrific, always full of locals from the early hours till late at night.

L'Affriolé

17 rue Malar

Tel: (01) 44 18 31 33

Open: Tue–Sat lunch and dinner

Inexpensive

Fantastic standard of food and the fixed price menu is a really good deal if you're on a budget, and the wine list is affordable too.

LA TOUR MAUBOURG

Hôtel des Invalides (1 min)

Esplanade des Invalides

Tel: *(01) 44 42 54 52; www.invalides.org*

Open: *not open to public*

Louis XIV built this magnificent building – completed in 1676 – as a hospital for wounded soldiers. There were up to 6,000 soldiers inside at any one time, but today only a handful live here and the buildings are used for government offices and three museums, the **Musée de l'Armée**, the **Dôme**

Thoumieux

79 rue St-Dominique

Tel: (01) 47 05 49 75

Open: daily, lunch and dinner

Moderate

Family-run bistro that has hardly changed since it opened in 1923, with hearty home-cooking and a warm welcome.

Church and **Napoleon's Tomb** (*see below*). The façade is 196m (645ft) long and four floors high; as you approach through the gardens, look at the top row of dormer windows surrounded by shields. Beyond the gate are the **Invalides Gardens**, which were designed in 1704 and have pathways lined by 17th- and 18th-century cannons.

Musée de l'Armée (2 mins)

Hôtel des Invalides, esplanade des Invalides
***Tel**: (01) 44 42 37 72; www.invalides.org*
***Open**: Apr–Sep daily 10am–6pm, Oct–Mar daily 10am–5pm, closed first Mon each month and holidays*
***Adm**: adults €7, students under-26 €5.50, under-18s free*

The biggest of the museums within the Hôtel des Invalides is the Army Museum, which has one of the largest collections of military items anywhere in the world. It goes right back to simple prehistoric clubs in the *Salle Préhistorique*, and there is also an *Oriental Room* and two rooms each devoted to one of the two world wars. There is a reconstruction of the room where Napoleon died in 1821, a collection of banners, models of French towns to show how fortifications developed, and a huge collection of armour, including horse armour. With the finely crafted guns, swords, shields and other items on display, a visit here can take longer than you might think.

Hôtel des Invalides

Dôme Church and Napoleon's Tomb

Dôme Church and Napoleon's Tomb (3 mins)

Hôtel des Invalides, esplanade des Invalides
***Tel**: (01) 45 55 37 69; www.invalides.org*
***Open**: Apr–Sep daily 10am–6pm, Oct–Mar daily 10am–5pm, closed first Mon each month and holidays*
***Adm**: included in ticket for Musée de l'Armée (**see** above)*

The golden dome that gleams over the Hôtel des Invalides marks the Dôme Church and the spot beneath which lies the tomb of Napoleon. The dome stands 107m (351ft) high and is a landmark throughout the city. Work on the church began in 1677 and continued for 27 years, although the Sun King, Louis XIV, only added the gilding to the dome in 1715. In 1840 Napoleon's body was brought here from St Helena and it rests today in a suitably impressive round crypt, inside six coffins beneath the painted ceiling under the dome, which shows the glory of Paradise.

Musée National Rodin (7 mins)

Hôtel Biron, 77 rue de Varenne
***Tel**: (01) 44 18 61 10; www.musee-rodin.fr*
***Open**: Apr–Sep Tue–Sun 9.30am–5.45pm, Oct–Mar Tue–Sun 9.30am–4.45pm*
***Adm**: adults €5 (€3 on Sun), 18–25s €3,*

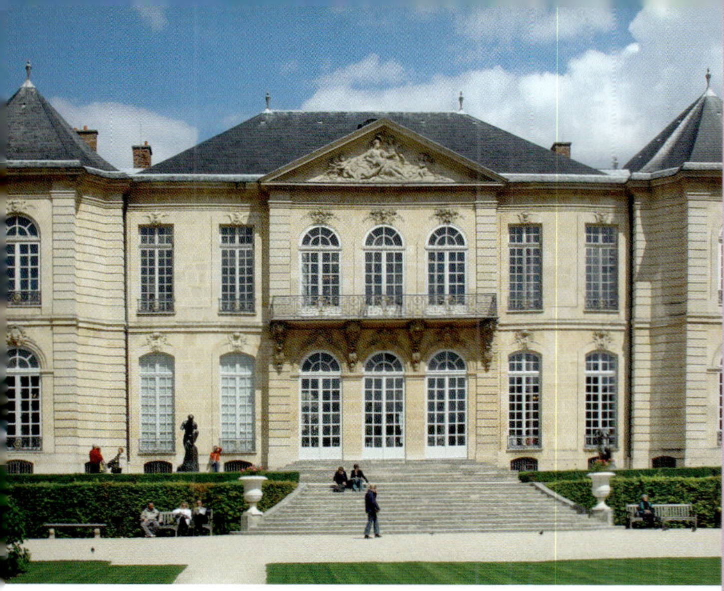

Musée National Rodin

under-18s free, first Sun each month free
Walking: (note that Varenne station on Line 13 is closer, if only visiting the Musée Rodin and not the other sights above.)

You can see the shining golden dome of the Dôme Church from within the large gardens of the Rodin Museum, which should be on everyone's list of things to see while in Paris.

The museum is in the Hôtel Biron, a beautiful 18th-century mansion where the sculptor spent the final nine years of his life. It was built in 1730 for the Duc de Biron, but in 1904 it was converted by the state into studios and apartments for artists to use. One of these was Auguste Rodin, who was given his studio and living quarters free of charge in return for agreeing to give his works to the nation after he died. On his death in 1917 the Hôtel was turned into the Musée Rodin.

The grounds comprise the third largest private gardens in Paris, which gives some idea of their size, and some of Rodin's most noted works, including *The Thinker* and *The Gates of Hell*, are displayed outside to great effect. Inside are familiar works including the ever-popular *The Kiss*, with items displayed more or less in chronological order. As well as the stunning sculptures, there are Rodin's sketches and watercolours, and his personal collection of works by such artists as Monet and Van Gogh. One room shows some of the powerful work by Camille Claudel, whose role as Rodin's model and lover tends to overshadow her own immense talents.

CONCORDE

See Line 1, p.22

Place de la Concorde p.22, Jeu de Paume p.23, Musée de L'Orangerie p.24

MADELEINE

Place de la Madeleine (1 min)

The place de la Madeleine isn't one of the city's greatest squares architecturally, but it's extremely popular with Parisians and visitors alike as here, and in the streets around, are some of the best speciality food shops in the city.

The square is dominated by the **church** in the centre (***see*** p.113), but you'll see many people worshipping in the windows of the gourmet shops on each side! The two best-known are **Fauchon** and **Hédiard**, which are general stores and sell almost anything that it's possible to eat and drink. They have tea rooms, so you can sample some of their goods, and Hédiard is especially interesting as it is renowned for importing exotic items to Paris, including many teas

Hédiard

21 place de la Madeleine

Tel: (01) 43 12 88 88; www.hediard.fr

Open: Mon–Sat 8.30am–9pm

Moderate

Looking in the windows of the exotic food shops on this square is sure to make you hungry. This old-fashioned tea room serves mouth-watering patisseries and a huge range of teas and coffees.

Place de la Madeleine

Il Cortile
37 rue Cambon
Tel: (01) 44 58 45 67
Open: Mon–Fri lunch and dinner
Expensive

The Italian food is sublime and ranges from innovative dishes to everyone's favourite desserts such as tiramisu and pannacotta.

and coffees, which you can find on the menu and so you can try before you buy.

But there are also some wonderful specialist stores on the square and in the immediate vicinity. It's a gourmet's treasure-hunt to meander up and down the streets that lead immediately off the square. There are, for example, shops devoted to mustard, to honey, to caviar, to cheese, to chocolate and to truffles (of the kind you dig up, not the chocolate variety).

On top of all that, on the eastern side of the square there is a small but very colourful **flower market**, held each day from Tuesday to Saturday. To add to the variety there are public toilets beneath the square, which were built in 1905 and are worth inspecting for their Art Nouveau design.

Église de la Madeleine (1 min)

Place de la Madeleine
***Tel**: (01) 44 51 69 00*
***Open**: daily 8am–6pm*
***Adm**: free*

The vast church that sits in the centre of the place de la Madeleine dates back to 1764, although it wasn't completed until 1842. In 1837 there were plans to turn it instead into Paris's first railway station, but

Église de la Madeleine

it eventually opened as a church, dedicated to St Mary Magdalene. Looking like some huge Greek temple, it has a frieze of the *Last Judgement* on the front and 52 supporting Corinthian pillars around it. It isn't the most graceful of buildings, and at times there have been various plans to turn it into all sorts of things: a bank, a theatre, a stock exchange and even a parliament building. But the church has survived, and is still used for weddings and funerals: Chopin and Marlene Dietrich had their burial services here.

Rue du Faubourg-St-Honoré (3 mins)

The rue du Faubourg-St-Honoré runs roughly parallel to the Champs-Élysées (***see*** p.19) and is one of the greatest – and most expensive – shopping streets in town. There are designer names almost everywhere you look, including Christian Lacroix, Pierre Cardin, Ungaro, Jaeger, Gucci, Dior, Sonia Rykiel, Versace, Yves Saint Laurent, Mont Blanc, Cartier, Karl Lagerfeld, Courrèges, Givenchy, Hermès, Guy Laroche and La Perla, to name just a few. Even if you can't afford to shop here, it's fun to look, and you're sure to see well-heeled (literally) Parisian ladies sweeping in and out the doors with husband, chauffeur or dog, or

Rue du Faubourg-St-Honoré

all three, trailing in their wake. In between all the high-fashion shops there are also galleries and antique shops, upmarket food shops, chocolate shops and wine merchants… and there are even a few 'ordinary' shops for the *hoi polloi* as well. Just to add to the allure, the French President lives at no. 55 Élysée Palace (***see*** p.131).

OPÉRA

Opéra National de Paris Garnier (1 min)

Place de l'Opéra
Tel*: (01) 40 01 22 63 for tours and information, (08) 36 69 78 68 for box office*
www.opera-de-paris.fr
Open*: daily 10am–5pm, telephone for tour times:* ***Adm****: tours €10; visit without a tour: adults €6, over-60s, students and 10–25s €4, under-10s free*

The ornate and very grand Paris Opera House is usually called the Opéra Garnier to distinguish it from the newer Opéra Bastille (***see*** p.40). Charles Garnier was the name of the unknown architect who won Napoleon III's competition to design a purpose-built opera house for the city in 1858. There had been opera in Paris long before that, but it had always been based in other theatres, including the theatre in the Palais-Royal. The new opera house was part of Napoleon III's grand vision for the redesign of the city centre, which was implemented by Baron Haussmann. It was finished in 1875, some 55 years after the idea was first mooted.

Garnier's design allowed for a large building and put the emphasis firmly on the stage and the back-stage areas, which meant that there is a comparatively small auditorium seating only 2,200 people. By contrast, you can fit 450 people on the stage, if needed, and there is a vast amount of space in the wings for changing sets around. Garnier's sumptuous interior uses five differently coloured marbles quarried in various parts of France to make a night

Opéra National de Paris Garnier

at the opera here an extremely splendid occasion. The *Grand Staircase* is one of the most striking features, made of white marble with the banisters in red and green.

The opera house can be visited, including the auditorium when there are no rehearsals, although behind-the-scenes tours cost a little more.

Musée de l'Opéra (1 min)

Opéra National de Paris Garnier, place de l'Opéra
Tel: *(01) 40 01 24 93*
Open: *daily 10am–6pm*
Adm: *adults €6, over-60s, students and 10–25s €4, under-10s free*

Also included in the admission price to the Opéra Garnier is its library and museum. The library was started in 1866, before the opera house was even finished, to document the building of the present house and to gather together material and memories from the opera company at its various homes going back to the 17th century. The museum has managed to acquire scores for every opera production, going back to 1669, and in all there are over 80,000 items in the collection.

Café de la Paix

12 boulevard des Capucines

Tel: (01) 40 07 36 36

Open: Daily for breakfast, lunch and dinner

Inexpensive

One of the great Paris cafés, whose grand style matches the nearby opera house, but don't let that put you off – it's popular with everybody, and you can pop in for a coffee and an ice cream as easily as for a three-course meal. But do pop in!

You can see Garnier's original drawings for the opera house, and a fascinating collection of models of stage sets for various productions. There is also a small gallery containing the opera house's own collection of paintings, which includes work by Renoir.

The museum also mounts temporary exhibitions on different operatic themes. When you enter the museum, you are using what was originally the Emperor's private entrance to the opera itself.

Musée de la Parfumerie Fragonard (2 mins)

9 rue Scribe
***Tel**: (01) 47 42 04 56*
***Open**: Apr–Oct daily 9am–5.30pm, Nov–Mar Mon–Sat 9am–5.30pm*
***Adm**: free*

Run by the perfume house of Fragonard, this museum naturally gives you the opportunity to buy some of its products in the gift shop at the end, but it is no hard sell and the museum itself provides a genuinely interesting account of the history of the perfume industry. There is a description of the perfume-making techniques of the ancient Egyptians, and the museum has a fine collection of Greek and Roman perfume bottles. There are also displays of more recent equipment,

Musée de la Parfumerie Fragonard

showing the perfume-making process to be similar to whisky-distilling; samples of the many exotic sources of the scents used in real perfumes are available. The art of the perfumer is also explained, with an example of a 'perfume organ', the desk at which the perfumer sits – with many different scents within easy reach around him – looking just like a person sitting playing an organ.

Musée de la Parfumerie Fragonard (second branch) (2 mins)

39 boulevard des Capucines
Tel: *(01) 42 60 37 14*
Open: *Mon–Sat 9am–5.30pm*
Adm: *free*

This is the second branch of the Fragonard Perfume Museum on the main road by the station. It is slightly different from the first though they cover much the same ground. As they are free and fairly close to each other, you may want to look at both. This branch has a lovely model of a perfume factory. There is a good range of gift items in the shop.

GRANDS BOULEVARDS

Musée Grévin (1 min)

10 boulevard Montmartre
Tel: *(01) 47 70 85 05; www.musee-grevin.com*
Open: *Mon–Fri 10am–6.30pm, Sat–Sun 10am–7pm*
Adm: *adults €16, students €13.80, 6–14s €9, under-6s free*

Many major cities have their branch of Madame Tussaud's, but Paris has an independent waxworks museum that can give the Madame a good run for her money. The Grévin Museum goes back to 1882 and was founded by Alfred Grévin, who was a sculptor and a cartoonist, and a journalist friend, Arthur Meyer. The tradition is kept up by the Académie Grévin, which meets twice a year to decide who's in and who's out – typical of the French to make it serious and fun at the same time.

Chartier

7 rue du Faubourg-Montmartre

Tel: (01) 47 70 86 29

Open: daily, lunch and dinner

Inexpensive

Everyone should eat at Chartier at least once, for its fantastic atmosphere, wonderful ornate dining room and cheap but good grub. There are often queues but they move quickly.

On display is a familiar clutch of movie and music stars, politicians and the British royal family. This being Paris, you also get a good number of more artistic types ranging from Rodin and Dali in their studios to fashion designer Jean-Paul Gaultier. There are plenty of historical scenes, too, including the trial of Joan of Arc and the killing of Henri IV and, naturally, plenty from the French Revolution starring Madame Guillotine. Then there's Madonna, Marilyn Monroe, Elton John, Elvis Presley, Hilary Clinton and many more...unless of course they have been melted down in the meantime.

Les Passages (1-2 mins)

Passage Verdeau, 9 rue de la Grange-Bateliere
Passage Jouffroy, 10–12 boulevard Montmartre
Passage des Panoramas, 11 boulevard Montmartre

Paris's *passages* are one of the city's joys for shoppers, and there are several of them in this area in particular. When they were at their peak, in the mid-19th century, there were over a hundred of them. Town planners created the shopping arcades that

Les Passages

run between streets in the early 19th century, when pedestrians were complaining about the problems caused by the increasing amount of horse-drawn traffic. The streets were still a muddle, with heavy traffic a fairly new phenomenon, and the mud and other deposits left by the horses and carriages were distinctly unpleasant.

Refuges were created by building shopping *passages*, where only pedestrians could go. They boomed and then faded again, as pavements came and horses went, but the *passages* have had a resurgence in the last few years as the intense traffic in city centres once again makes shoppers want to seek havens from the noise.

A close look at a good street map will show where these treasures are, as it is very easy to miss some of the smaller ones when walking quickly by. Look for the name *passage* or *galerie*. Some of them are beautiful glass and metal constructions, worthy of Gustave Eiffel himself, and they tend to be places where specialist shops – milliners, stamp sellers, postcard shops, book dealers, doll's houses and others – can cling on in the city centre, not totally driven out by high rents.

Some of the *passages* also offer good eating options, so if you are roaming around looking for somewhere to have a meal, don't forget to look along here. They have everything from *chic* to cheap and cheerful.

FILLES DU CALVAIRE

Cirque d'Hiver Bouglione (1 min)

110 rue Amelot
Tel: *(01) 47 00 12 25; www.cirquedhiver.com*
Open: *Oct–Jan, ring for show times*
Adm: *€10–35*

If you're having a drink in the Clown Bar or any of the other cafés or bars in the area, don't be surprised if a real clown walks in. This is the home of Paris's Winter Circus, and the circus workers sometimes pop out

Clown Bar

114 rue Amelot

Tel: (01) 43 55 87 35

Open: Mon–Sat lunch and dinner, Sun dinner

Inexpensive

The Clown Bar has circus decoration, old-fashioned tables, a zinc bar but a very modern look. Now more restaurant than bar, it is still a fun place to call in for a drink, and worth knowing about if you're in the area on Sunday evenings, when lots of eating places are closed.

for something to fortify them during rehearsals or performances. Circuses are regarded more seriously in France than in other countries, and the performers are looked on as artists. The *Cirque d'Hiver* (Winter Circus) has a permanent home here – not a tent but a beautiful 19th-century building, where the circus plays from October to January. Even when it's closed the building itself is worth a look, as is the Clown Bar, which is full of circus fun.

BASTILLE

***See* Line 1, p.40**

L'Opéra p.40, Canal St-Martin p.41, Richard Lenoir Market p.42, Rue de Lappe p.42, Rue du Faubourg-St-Antoine p.42, Promenade Plantée p.43, Viaduc des Arts p.44, Place des Vosges p.44, Maison de Victor Hugo p.45

LEDRU-ROLLIN

Aligre Market (5 mins)

Place d'Aligre
***Open**: daily*

Every morning except Monday, until about 1pm, the Aligre Market is buzzing. It's one of the best in the city, not in terms of its size but in the variety of things here, the atmosphere and the fact that it is actually three markets in one. To get to the Aligre market walk east along the main street, rue du Faubourg-St-Antoine, when you come out of the Métro station, and turn right down rue de Cotte. Pay a visit and you might see why this has been described as 'the Notre-Dame of markets'.

For the real quality produce, go inside the covered part of the market, the Beauveau St-Antoine, itself a lovely old building. Some of the stalls are pretty old, too, and you will find traditional butchers and suppliers of game. Expect to see wild boar or pheasants hanging from the ceiling, or whatever else is in season. There are stalls where you can buy fish, foie gras, truffles, pâtés, cheeses, wines and other gourmet delights. If you have a foodie friend back home and know they'd

Fruit and vegetables, Aligre Market

appreciate a real treat, you're sure to find something here at the Aligre, though you'll probably have to buy two and keep one for yourself. This is the place where the local chefs come to get the specialities on their menus, and when something special is in short supply or a particularly good example comes in, like truffles, then you might find the stallholder selling it by auction to the highest bidder.

Outside the covered market is the more regular produce market, with lots of fruit and vegetable stalls. Many of these are run by North Africans, who sell lots of exotic imported foodstuffs as well as the more usual items. Prices are good – there's no comparison with the gourmet stuff inside the covered market. On Sunday morning the square and streets around it get especially lively.

Finally there is also a small flea market. People sell clothes and jewellery, and some sell fabrics. Some of the streetwise fashion designers come here, looking for inspiration or just the right piece of material they need.

The buzz of the market spills over into the surrounding streets, where you'll find some excellent bakers, a few good eating places, and one of the stallholders' favourite bars, the Baron Rouge. As the market starts to empty, the bar starts to fill. Le Pain au Naturel at 5 place d'Aligre is an organic bakery, which opened in 1997 and makes such tasty treats as bread with basil or dried apricots. Another one to try is

Le Square Trousseau

1 rue Antoine-Vollon

Tel: (01) 43 43 06 00

Open: Tue–Sat lunch and dinner

Moderate

Yet another restaurant with a wonderful interior, where it's a feast for the eyes as well. It dates back to the 1900s, but the menu is resolutely modern, appealing to the eclectic mix of locals in this fashionable area. A place to savour, not snack.

Cheese, Aligre Market

Bazin at 85 bis rue de Charenton, on one of the streets running down from the market. This is also a speciality baker, and his specialities include rye bread baked with almonds, hazelnuts, walnuts and raisins. How can you not want to taste that?

Le Baron Rouge

1 rue Théophile-Roussel

Tel: (01) 43 43 14 32

Open: Mon–Sat lunch and dinner, Sun lunch, but cold food available all day

Inexpensive

The Baron Rouge is a 'must-visit' wine bar, which you'll recognize by the upturned wine barrels acting as tables on the pavement outside. It oozes atmosphere; wines are available by the glass and there is a simple but tasty little food menu.

29 avenue Rapp

LINE 9

PONT DE SÈVRES – MAIRIE DE MONTREUI

Line 9 is one of the 'newer' lines, dating back only to 1922. In 1934 it was extended to what is still its southwest terminus Pont de Sèvres, and in 1937 to what remains its eastern terminus, Mairie de Montreuil. The line of this route is 19.6k (12.25 miles) long has remained unchanged for almost 70 years. For part of its length, Line 9 runs by the River Seine - where there are a few unusual museums worth checking ou and elsewhere it will take you from one extreme to the othe from the Presidential Palace to the Sewers.

TROCADÉRO

Palais de Chaîllot, ***see*** p.84

Cité de l'Architecture et du Patrimoine, ***see*** p.85

Musée de l'Homme ***see*** p.85

Musée de la Marine, ***see*** p.86

Jardins du Trocadéro, ***see*** p.86

IÉNA

Musée Nationale des Arts Asiatiques Guimet 126

Musée de la Mode et du Costume 127

Musée d'Art Moderne de la Ville de Paris 128

ALMA-MARCEAU

Les Égouts (The Sewers) 129

No. 29 Avenue Rapp 130

FRANKLIN D. ROOSEVELT

Franklin D. Roosevelt Métro station, ***see*** p.17

Avenue Montaigne, ***see*** p.17

Avenue Matignon, ***see*** p.18

Palais de la Découverte, ***see*** p.18

ST-PHILIPPE-DU-ROULE

MIROMESNIL

Palais de l'Élysée 131

ST-AUGUSTIN

HAVRE-CAUMARTIN

CHAUSSÉE D'ANTIN-LA FAYETTE

RICHELIEU-DROUOT

GRANDS BOULEVARDS

Musée Grevin, ***see*** p.118

Les Passages, ***see*** p.119

TROCADÉRO

See Line 6, p.84

Palais de Chaillot p.84, Cité de l'Architecture et du Patrimoine p.85, Musée de l'Homme p.85, Musée de la Marine p.86, Jardins du Trocadéro p.86

IÉNA

Musée Nationale des Arts Asiatiques Guimet (1 min)

6 place d'Iéna
***Tel**: (01) 56 52 53 00; www.museeguimet.fr*
***Open**: Wed–Mon 10am–6pm*
***Adm**: adults €7, students, 18–25s and on Sun €5, under-18s free, first Sun each month free*

Although Paris's museums naturally have a very strong focus on French art, there are other collections that highlight art from other countries and civilizations, and this is one of the best. It reopened a few years ago after several years of renovation and the result is that the 45,000 objects in the collection are better organized and displayed than ever.

Musée Nationale des Arts Asiatiques Guimet

Fakhr El Dine

30 rue de Longchamp

Tel: (01) 47 27 90 00; www.fakhreldine.com

Open: Daily, lunch and dinner

Moderate

This stylish Lebanese restaurant is definitely recommended, as the tasty and subtle Middle Eastern cuisine blends just perfectly with a bit of French sophistication.

Emile Guimet was an industrialist from Lyon who had a fascination for the arts and cultures of Asia. He originally displayed his collection in his home city, before it was transferred to Paris in 1884 where it became one of the world's leading collections of Asiatic art. One of the highlights is the Cambodian art, including some huge sculptures from Khmer temples.

There are strong collections from Japan and China, two countries that Guimet was especially interested in, and the whole collection was enhanced by the addition of items from the Louvre's collection (***see*** p.31). There are objects from Afghanistan, India and Pakistan, and all the southeast Asian countries, going as far back as Neolithic times. Mirrors, jewellery, paintings, ceramics, statues, embroidery… allow plenty of time for a visit.

Musée de la Mode et du Costume (2 mins)

Palais Galliéra, 10 avenue Pierre 1er de Serbie
Tel*: (01) 56 52 86 00*
Open*: Tue–Sun 10am–6pm*
Adm*: adults €7, over-60s €5.50, 13–26s €3.50, under-13s free*

Also known as the Musée de la Mode de la Ville de Paris and the Musée Galliéra, this complements the Musée de la Mode at du Textile (***see*** p.29). Housed in a rather grand Renaissance-style mansion dating from 1892 and originally built for the Duchesse Maria de Ferrari Galliéra, it also contains the offices of the French state's national fashion and costume collection, which runs to some 100,000 items from the 18th century right through to the very latest designers, who provide samples of their work for these archives.

Because of the size of the collection and the fragility of some of the earlier items, there are just two or three major displays each year in the two ground-floor rooms. Displays might cover a particular designer, or a period, or the evolution of a particular style or item. Each September there is a display called *Modes à Suivre* (Fashions to Follow) highlighting the new styles of up-and-coming designers at the same time as they go on sale in the shops.

Musée d'Art Moderne de la Ville de Paris (2 mins)

11 avenue du Président-Wilson
Tel*: (01) 53 67 40 00;*
www.paris.fr/musees/MAMVP/default.htm
Open*: Tue–Fri 10am–5.30pm, Sat–Sun 10am–7pm*
Adm*: free, charge for special exhibitions*

This is the state collection of 20th-century art, housed in the east wing of the Palais de Tokyo, which was built in the 1930s. It is currently being renovated and is due to reopen sometime in 2005. In the meantime, look out for special exhibitions around the city as various aspects of a wonderful collection have been displayed around Paris in the town halls of the different districts. Also, check out the website for exhibitions *les lieux hors des murs*, 'outside these walls'. The part of the collection devoted to contemporary art can also be found in the **Couvent des Cordeliers** (15 rue de l'École de Médecine; Métro: Odéon) along with a series of lectures and performances.

When the museum reopens it will contain a choice selection of modern art with names such as Matisse, Dufy, André Breton, Picasso, Modigliani, Braque and Chagall, and all the leading modern movements such as Cubism, Surrealism, Dada, Abstract and especially the

Musée d'Art Moderne de la Ville de Paris

Fauvres. Before renovation an entire room had been devoted to the Matisse collection, and the most striking display was Raoul Dufy's mural, *The Spirit of Electricity*, created for the 1937 World Fair to tell the story of electricity; it fills an entire curved wall, measuring some 60m x 10m (197ft x 33ft).

Maison Blanche

15 ave. Montaigne

Tel: (01) 47 23 55 99

Open: daily, lunch and dinner

Expensive

Situated above the Théâtre des Champs-Elysées, this ultra-smart spot serves food to die for but the lunchtime menu makes it more affordable - just!

ALMA-MARCEAU

Les Égouts (The Sewers) (4 mins)

Entrance on the left bank by the Pont de l'Alma

***Tel**: (01) 53 68 27 81*

***Open**: Sat–Wed 11am–4pm*

***Adm**: adults €3.80, over-60s and students €3.05, 5–12s €2.30, under-5s free*

If one of the essentials of Paris is taking a trip to the top of the Eiffel Tower (***see** p.87*), another is descending into the world of the sewers. One of the fascinations is seeing that the sewers are named like the streets, with the familiar little blue-and-white signs telling the underground workers exactly which street they are working beneath.

Most people know that in the latter half of the 19th century, the designer and architect Baron Haussmann transformed Paris, creating the wide boulevards and geometrical street layouts that help give it the graceful look with which we are so familiar. What fewer people know is that, at the same time, he was also designing the sewer system, as he knew that no city could be modern and stylish if it didn't also function in a practical way. The new and comprehensive sewer system helped to ventilate and sanitize Paris and, in many ways, is an even greater achievement than what Haussmann did above ground.

Naturally, only part of the sewer system is on display and the entrance is across the pont de l'Alma from the Métro station, on the left down the stairs.

The tours are guided and led by one of the city's retired sewerage workers and are utterly fascinating. They last for an hour and begin with an audiovisual show, but there's also time to browse the fascinating history displays, which give astonishing statistics.

The Paris sewer tunnels extend some 2100km (1300 miles) in all, and if placed end to end would transport Paris's sewage all the way to Istanbul. As you walk around the part of the system that has been opened to visitors you can see the world that exists beneath the feet and the streets of the city. The telephone cables are down here, the pipes for the vital services and the cable networks, as well as the water and effluent pipes.

There's also a great deal of historical interest, as the sewers have been used both by the French resistance fighters and by the occupying Germans during World War II. They also feature in Victor Hugo's book *Les Misérables* as well as in *Phantom of the Opera*.

There are old sewerage machines on display as well as suggestions about how the sewers of the future will operate. The displays are in French and English and include old photographs and drawings and information on the various, sometimes bizarre, items that turn up in the system from time to time. There's a display on the great sewerage flood in 1802, before the modern system was designed to cope with such things, and it doesn't take much to imagine the rather unappealing consequences of the sewerage system being flooded. The whole experience is suitably dark and dank, though in no way dangerous or unpleasant. Children, naturally, love it.

No.29 avenue Rapp (8 mins)

Head southwest from the entrance to the sewers along avenue Rapp, and watch out on the left-hand side for no. 29 – though it's rather hard to miss. The front is one of the most flamboyant and exotic buildings in Paris. It's considered to be one of the best examples of Art Nouveau anywhere in the world, and was one of Salvador Dali's favourite buildings. Its designer, Jules

No. 29 avenue Rapp

Lavirotte, won first prize at the 1901 *Concours des Façades de la Ville de Paris* competition for this building. Take a close look at the female figures, animals and flowers that weave their way up the front. Dali also regarded it as one of the most erotic building designs he had ever seen.

FRANKLIN D. ROOSEVELT

See Line 1, p.17

Franklin D. Roosevelt Métro station p.17, Avenue Montaigne p.17, Avenue Matignon p.18, Palais de la Découverte p.18

MIROMESNIL

Palais de l'Élysée (4 mins)

55 rue du Faubourg-St-Honoré
***Open**: not open to the public (but **see** below)*

Heading north from the Métro along the avenue Marigny you reach the Élysée Palace, home of the French president. Note that you should walk along the left-hand side of the road as the security guards don't like people walking along the right-hand side, by the palace walls.

The palace was built in 1718 and designed by Armande-Claude Mollet for the Count of Évreux, and then the Marquise de Pompadour, whose wife, Madame de Pompadour, was the mistress of Louis XV, bought it in 1753. She enlarged the building

Palais de l'Élysée

and had the gardens extended all the way to the Champs-Élysées (*__see__* p.19). After the French Revolution it was turned into both a government printing works and a dance hall!

In the 19th century it became the home of Napoleon's sister, Caroline Murat. Later, Napoleon's wife, the Empress Josephine, moved in after her divorce from the Emperor and, on 22 June 1815, the Emperor found himself signing his second abdication here after his defeat at the Battle of Waterloo. Later still, in 1851, it was home to his nephew, Napoleon III, when he was plotting his coup. Should you be fortunate enough to see inside, you will see the two rooms that have been preserved from that time, the *Salon Murat* and the *Salon d'Argent*. Murat was the name of Caroline's husband, and *Salon d'Argent* means the Room of Silver.

It then had rather a chequered history, as both a restaurant and the site of a fairground, before regaining its dignity in 1873 when it became the official residence of the President of France in 1873.

It is very much a working government headquarters, and is where the French ministers meet every Wednesday, with their council chamber (the Salon Murat)

Le Bistrot du Sommelier

97 boulevard Haussmann

Tel: (01) 42 65 24 85; www.bistrotdusommelier.com

Open: Mon–Fri lunch and dinner

Expensive

Smart restaurant owned by one of the city's best sommeliers, so not cheap but worth a splurge when you're in this upmarket district. The fixed-price lunch menu is more affordable.

René de Saint-Ouen

111 boulevard Haussmann

Tel: (01) 42 65 06 25

Open: Mon–Sat, 7am–8pm

Inexpensive

If you've been to see the Presidential Palace, why not call in at the bakery where several French Presidents have bought their baguettes? It's a good place to know about in this expensive area, as an alternative to a sit-down meal, and children will love the little loaves made in the shapes of birds and animals.

being one of the rooms normally open to the public on the one day a year that the palace throws open its doors.

The French President still lives here when he is in Paris, in apartments on the first floor on the western side of the building – hence the high security and attention you'll get should you wander too close to the wall. These modern apartments were designed by the modern French designer, Philippe Starck. It is here that visiting dignitaries stay and the guards outside are even more alert when there are overseas guests, following in the footsteps of earlier visitors, including the Duke of Wellington, Czar Alexander I and Queen Victoria.

If you are keen to see inside the Palace, visit Paris during the third weekend of September. This is when the annual *Journées du Patrimoine* (Patrimony Days) take place, and buildings usually closed to the public give free admission. The Élysée Palace is one of the most popular of these and the tour takes in the front of the building, about a dozen of the rooms, and gives you chance to glimpse the gardens. There isn't a guide, but a free leaflet in French is provided to identify what you're seeing. The doors usually open at 10am, but you will need to be dedicated as queues start to form hours before and you will almost certainly be in for a long wait.

GRANDS BOULEVARDS

***See* Line 8, p.118**

Musée Grevin p.118, Les Passages p.119

Musée de Cluny

LINE 10

BOULOGNE PONT DE ST-CLOUD – GARE D'AUSTERLITZ

When Line 10 was opened in 1923, it was only intended to serve the area south of the River Seine, running through much of the popular Left Bank district. In the late 1930s, it was extended under the river at its eastern end, with the final extension as far as Boulogne-Pont de St-Cloud only being opened in 1981. The whole line runs underground. Line 10 is very useful for visiting the popular Left Bank as it takes in the university district of the Sorbonne; the wonderful Cluny Museum; the Panthéon, where the great and the good of Paris are entombed; and the Jardin des Plantes, one of the Parisians' favourite city centre parks, which has lots of different attractions.

ODÉON

See Line 4, p.70

Le Procope p.70, Cour du Commerce St-André p.71, Cour de Rohan p.71, Musée de la Monnaie de Paris p.71, Rue de l'Odéon p.71

CLUNY LA SORBONNE

Musée de Cluny (2 mins)

6 place Paul-Painlevé
***Tel**: (01) 53 73 78 00; www.musee-moyenage.fr*
***Open**: Wed–Mon 9.15am–5.45pm*
***Adm**: adults €5.55 (€4 on Sun), 18–25s €4, under-18s free and free first Sun each month*

When you walk through the imposing Gothic courtyard that marks the entrance to the Musée de Cluny, you are following in some famous footsteps. It was built in the 15th century as the Hôtel de Cluny, the Paris home for well-to-do Benedictine monks from Cluny in Burgundy and, among later guests and residents, were King James V of Scotland and Mary Tudor, the sister of Henry VIII, who was married to Louis XII of France for three short months in October 1514. In the 19th century it was bought by Alexandre du

Bouillon Racine

3 rue Racine

Tel: (01) 44 32 15 60

Open: Daily, lunch and dinner

Walking time: 2 mins

Moderate

The Art Nouveau interior dating from 1906 makes this worth thinking about for a lunch or dinner stop, and it's not surprising this is a listed historic building. The menu is traditional French, very meaty, but tends to cater more for the tourist trade than for local diners.

Musée de Cluny

Somme, an art collector whose collection forms the basis for what is, to give it its full title, the Musée National du Moyen Âge – Thermes de Cluny: the National Museum of the Middle Ages and the Baths of Cluny.

The Gallo-Roman baths are the oldest but not necessarily the most interesting aspect of the museum. They date back to the second century AD and you can see what remains of the huge cold baths, the *frigidarium*, incorporated into one of the ground floor rooms of the museum. In this same room is also Paris's oldest known sculpture, dating from 30 AD.

The large collection of almost 25,000 items from the Middle Ages fascinates most visitors, in particular the tapestries, and especially the six tapestries known as, 'The Lady and the Unicorn', which inspired the novel of the same name by Tracy Chevalier (who also wrote *Girl with a Pearl Earring*, about the Dutch painter, Vermeer). These 15th-century tapestries were from Holland, made from silk and wool, and are wonderfully detailed and intriguing in their imagery.

See also Line 4, St-Michel p.69
Boulevard St-Michel p.69, St-Séverin p.69, St-Julien-le-Pauvre p.70

CARDINAL LEMOINE

St-Etienne-du-Mont

St-Etienne-du-Mont (4 mins)

Place Ste-Geneviève
Tel: *(01) 43 54 11 79*
Open: *Mon noon–6.30pm, Tue–Fri 8am–7.30pm, Sat 9am–noon and 2–6.30pm, Sun 9am–noon and 2.30–6.30pm*
Adm: *free*

This church, although dwarfed by its near neighbour, the great Panthéon (***see*** p.138), is still worth a visit. It houses the remains of Racine and Pascal, and has a shrine to Saint Geneviève, the patron saint of Paris. The shrine is here because there was an abbey to Saint Geneviève on this site, before the construction of the church began in 1492. It took 134 years to complete, hence the strange mix of architectural styles. It also has a lovely and detailed rood screen, some vivid stained glass and a 16th-century belfry.

Panthéon (5 mins)

Place du Panthéon
Tel: *(01) 44 32 18 00*
Open: *Apr–Sep daily 10am–6.30pm, Oct–Mar daily 10am–6pm*
Adm: *adults €7, 18–25s €4.50, under-18s free*

The moment you set eyes on the Panthéon, especially if approaching from the front, you know you are in the presence of a very significant building. And so it is, for here are buried some of France's greatest and most famous citizens, including Marie Curie, Louis Braille and Voltaire.

Originally built as a church by Louis XV to celebrate his recovery from a serious case of gout in 1744, the Panthéon wasn't finished until 1790. It was dedicated to the patron saint of the city, Sainte Geneviève, and modelled (though not well) on the Pantheon in Rome, hence the name. The walls are covered with historical and mythological scenes, many by the 19th-century artist Puvis de Chavannes.

To be dignified with a burial in the here is a great honour, accorded to some people – for example the author Émile Zola – only

Fresco of Sainte Geneviève, Panthéon

The Panthéon

after their death. They are then re-buried here with great ceremony, as happened most recently (on 29 November 2002) to Alexandre Dumas, author of *The Three Musketeers*. The Panthéon has several great writers buried in its vast crypt, including Dumas, Hugo, Rousseau and Zola.

There are scientists here too, such as Louis Braille, who invented the reading system for the blind, and the scientists Marie and Pierre Curie. The Panthéon was also the scene of a great scientific experiment, 'Foucault's Pendulum'. The scientist Foucault suspended a giant pendulum directly under the dome of the Panthéon, which he set swinging in a straight line. As the pendulum swung, it became clear that its path over the floor was slowly changing. Foucault maintained correctly that as the pendulum was not moving, it must be the earth that was rotating. A replica of the pendulum is still swinging today.

Les Quatre et Une Saveurs

72 rue du Cardinal-Lemoine

Tel: (01) 43 26 88 80

Open: Sun–Fri lunch, Sat–Thu dinner

Moderate

Fantastically tasty vegetarian, organic dishes in this non-smoking restaurant, though they do have fish on the menu too, and everything is freshly cooked.

JUSSIEU

Arènes de Lutèce (2 mins)

Rue de Navarre
***Open**: summer daily 8am–10pm, winter daily 8am–5.30pm*
***Adm**: free*

Paris is not exactly renowned for its Roman remains, and Roman amphitheatre dating from the second-century AD is one of only two in the city, along with the Roman baths at the Cluny Museum (***see** p.136*). The arena was destroyed in AD 280 and rediscovered in 1869; the novelist Victor Hugo, who campaigned successfully for the restoration of Notre-Dame (***see** p.67*) also worked to have this arena restored. The original was 35 rows high and could hold 10,000 people. Attractions included theatrical performances, and gladiator and wild animal battles. A few stone seats are all that remain, and the arena is used now mainly as a small park, with a playground, benches and gardens all around. The name comes from the Roman name for Paris, *Lutetia*.

Arènes de Lutèce

Le Buisson Ardent

25 rue Jussieu

Tel: (01) 43 54 93 02

Open: Mon–Fri lunch and dinner

Moderate

Friendly neighbourhood bistro doing better than average food, with a more adventurous menu in the evenings. Good bet for a cheap fixed-price lunch.

Jardin des Plantes

Jardin des Plantes (2 mins)

57 rue Cuvier
***Open**: daily 7.15am–sunset*
***Adm**: free*

The royal medicinal herb gardens that were planted here in 1626 give their name to this whole district as well as to the large park, which has long been a Parisian favourite. It was established by Jean Hérouard and Guy de la Brosse, who were the physicians to Louis XIII, and in 1640, the King's private pharmacy was opened to the public.

Almost 400 years later, the *Jardin* is as popular as ever, and is still used both as a public park and as a research centre for plants – there are an estimated 10,000 different species here. There's also a **menagerie**, a **natural history museum**, several **speciality gardens**, and trees that are well over 200 years old.

One such tree is the Sophora of Japan, which is known to have been planted in 1747 from seeds sent to the *Jardin* by a Jesuit naturalist. It first flowered in 1777 and still flowers today. Not quite as old, at a mere 150 years, is the *Gingko biloba*, but because the species coexisted with the dinosaurs 125 million years ago, it is nicknamed the 'Dinosaur Tree'. A model of a real dinosaur

Natural History Museum

stands outside the Palaeontology Gallery of the Natural History Museum, and is a great favourite with children as it is designed so that they can climb all over it.

Natural History Museum (2 mins)

Jardin des Plantes
***Tel**: (01) 40 79 30 00; www.mnhn.fr*
***Open**: Wed–Mon 10am–6pm*
***Adm**: adults €7, students, 3–12s €5, under-3s free*

The National Museum of Natural History is housed in several buildings – the star attraction is a beautifully refurbished 19th-century building of glass and steel, archetypal Parisian architecture, containing the *Grand Evolution Gallery*. Inside this large building, a little like a high-domed railway station, elephants, giraffes, apes and other animals stride across an African savannah, while above them is suspended a huge whale skeleton and all around are sound effects and displays that tell the whole wonderful story of the development of life on earth. There are several floors, including a basement where the mysteries of the ocean are revealed, and on the first floor is an interactive section for children.

If the day is wet, any family can safely head here and know that everyone will be captivated. There are other buildings with departments of anatomy, entomology, mineralogy, palaeobotany and palaeontology, interesting enough, but if time is tight visit the Evolution Gallery first.

Paris Zoo (*La Ménagerie*) (2 mins)

Jardin des Plantes
Tel*: (01) 44 05 72 72*
Open*: Daily 9am–6.30pm (closes 5.30pm in winter)*
Adm*: adults €6, students, 4–18s and over-60s €3, under-4s free*

The ménagerie is the oldest zoo in France, and in places could do with the kind of modernizing restoration that is being given to the city's art galleries. But there are also areas where the animals roam freely, and a great favourite with everyone is the *Microzoo*. No problems of space here, as you explore the world of insects, spiders and anything else that looks fascinating or scary under a microscope.

Centre Georges Pompidou

LINE 11

CHÂTELET – MAIRIE DES LILAS

You can ride the entire length of Line 11 in 15 minutes, as it is only 6.3km long – less than four miles, and all underground. The line is often used to test out new trains. Because it's one of the newer lines, and the first section was only opened in 1935, it runs underneath the existing lines, which is why many of the stations have long escalators. It also required a large number of sharp curves and steep gradients to fit it into the network and link with other stations, so it is an ideal testing ground for innovations.

CHÂTELET

Les Halles, ***see*** Les Halles p.62

Église St-Eustache, ***see*** Les Halles p.62

HÔTEL DE VILLE

Hôtel de Ville 146

Cloître des Billettes 147

Église Saint Merri 147

RAMBUTEAU

Centre Georges Pompidou 148

Notre-Dame-des-Blancs-Manteaux 150

Musée d'Art et d'Histoire du Judaïsme 150

Musée de la Chasse et de la Nature 152

ARTS ET MÉTIERS

RÉPUBLIQUE

GONCOURT

BELLEVILLE

Musée Edith Piaf, ***see*** p.57

CHÂTELET

See Line 4, Les Halles, p.62

Les Halles p.62, Église St-Eustache p.62

HOTEL DE VILLE

Hôtel de Ville (1 min)

Place de l'Hôtel de Ville, rue de Rivoli
***Tel**: (01) 42 76 50 49*
***Open**: public tour Mon 10.30am only, book in advance*
***Adm**: free*

The middle section of the impressive façade of the Paris Town Hall is a copy of the original building, which dated back to 1533, but was burned down during the Paris Commune of 1871. The present building was put up soon after but is closed to the public apart from one weekly guided tour, which needs to be booked in advance. The area in front of the Town Hall is a pleasant traffic-free zone, and it's worth taking a little time out to admire the fountains, the statues on the front of the building, the decorated stonework and the turreted roof.

Hôtel de Ville

Cloître des Billettes

Cloître des Billettes (3 mins)

24 rue des Archives
Tel: *(01) 42 72 38 79*
Open: *Sun 10am–noon, Thu 6–7.30pm (church for services only), cloister open during exhibitions (phone to check)*
Adm: *free*

This cloister was once part of a medieval church next door, which was destroyed, but the cloisters, dating from 1427, still survive and are the only ones left in Paris. They are still in use today as an effective setting for changing art exhibitions. If you want to check the opening times and find out what's on, look in a listings magazine under exhibitions rather than churches.

Église Saint Merri (3 mins)

78 rue Saint-Martin
Tel: *(01) 42 71 93 93*
Open: *Daily, 9am-7pm*

Saint Merri, just south of the Pompidou centre (***see** below*) has changed a lot over the years. Originally built in the 9th century and named for St Médard who was buried in Paris in 700 AD, it was rebuilt in 1220 and again in 1552, in Flamboyant Gothic style.

Inevitably, the gothic decoration was meddled with in the 18th century and replaced with Baroque elements. Although its statues were destroyed during the Revolution, the church survived as a powder factory. It was reinstated in the 19th century and the chapels decorated. A small turret on the left contains the oldest bell in Paris, dating from 1331. Every Saturday, there are free classical concerts at 9pm.

RAMBUTEAU

Centre Georges Pompidou (1 min)

Rue St-Martin
***Tel**: (01) 44 78 12 33; www.centrepompidou.fr*
***Open**: Wed–Mon 11am–9pm (some exhibitions till 11pm)*
***Adm**: adults €5.50, 18–26s €3.50, under-18s free; additional payment for some exhibitions, day pass also available*

Of all the modern buildings in Paris, the magnet for visitors is the still startling Pompidou Centre. It was a jolt to the senses when it opened in 1977, but unlike much 1970s' architecture the Pompidou Centre remains a striking creation and a popular building with Parisians, who make full use of its many facilities. Visitors tend to want to see the building itself, and the **Modern Art Museum**, which occupies just one floor.

The Centre was designed by acclaimed architects Richard Rogers and Renzo Piano, who surprised everyone – especially local people – by seeming to turn the building inside out. Instead of hiding the electricity and other utilities, they ran them through boldly coloured pipes on the outside of the building. The green pipes carry the water supply, the blue ones the air-conditioning and the yellow ones feed electricity to the building. The main escalator is also stuck on the front of the building in a plexi-glass tube, climbing its way to the top and colour-coded red underneath.

In front of the Centre is an open space where people meet, relax and watch the fire-eaters, performance artists and other

Georges

6th Floor, Centre Georges Pompidou

Tel: (01) 44 78 47 99

Open: Wed–Mon noon–2am

Walking time: 5 mins

Expensive

Stylish French–Asian restaurant on top of the Pompidou Centre; you'll need to get there early for the tables with the best rooftop views, or slip in mid-afternoon for a coffee and a snack.

Centre Georges Pompidou

buskers who come here to entertain the crowds. Nearby is the Stravinsky Fountain, where multicoloured sculptures inspired by Stravinsky's *The Firebird* entertain the crowds by spraying water around the place.

As you enter the Centre there's an excellent bookshop and a row of ticket kiosks, and you need to take a little time to decide what you actually want to buy tickets for. There's a cinema and a library as well as temporary exhibitions and the permanent Musée National d'Art Moderne (National Museum of Modern Art).

The Modern Art Museum should be top of the list. This works in conjunction with the other major Paris museums by concentrating on art from 1905 onwards; it includes photography, video, architecture and mixed media artists. Some of the world's great names are here – Picasso, Braque, Warhol, Pollock, Miro, Matisse – and by keeping right up-to-date, perhaps some of the great names of the future too. The Centre has about 50,000 items in its collection, of which only a fraction are on display at any one time.

By continuing up the building you can reach the Georges restaurant, a great place to eat, and if you're not hungry then just take in the view from the top of the Centre. Here you can marvel at this exciting modern building, while looking for Paris's other notable landmarks, including Notre-Dame (***see*** p.67) and the Eiffel Tower (***see*** p.87), which create a historical panorama.

Notre-Dame-des-Blancs-Manteaux (3 mins)

12 Rue des Blancs Manteaux
Tel*: (01) 42 72 09 37*
Open*: 10am–12.45pm*
Adm*: free*

This church takes its name from the white cloaks ('blancs manteaux') of the 13th-century monks who first lived on this site. Before that, it was known as the 'Petite-Parcheminerie' or 'Vieille-Parcheminerie' on account of the parchment makers who lived along here. The church itself dates from 1685 and is notable for its 18th-century Flemish pulpit and its organ, built by one of the most renowned 20th-century organ makers, Alfred Kern, on which recitals are given every week.

Le Potager du Marais

22 rue Rambuteau

Tel: (01) 44 54 00 31

Open: daily, lunch and dinner

Inexpensive

French cuisine doesn't cater too well for vegetarians but this organic place offers incredibly tasty and inexpensive dishes, in a busy bistro-like atmosphere. Non-veggies should also give it a try – it really is that good.

Musée d'Art et d'Histoire du Judaïsme (2 mins)

Hôtel de St-Aignan, 71 rue du Temple
Tel*: (01) 53 01 86 60; www.mahj.org*
Open*: Mon–Fri 11am–6pm, Sun 10am–6pm, Sat and some Jewish holidays closed*
Adm*: adults €6.10, students and 18–26s €3.80, under-18s free*

It's appropriate that in 1998 this museum was re-housed here from its former quarters, as the Hôtel itself is part of the Jewish history in Paris. In the 19th century Jewish immigrants who had recently arrived from Eastern Europe lived here, in the heart of the Jewish quarter of the city (***see*** *also*, Line 1, St-Paul, a little further east). It was still being used to welcome

Musée d'Art et d'Histoire du Judaïsme

Le Hangar

12 impasse Berthaud

Tel: (01) 42 74 55 44

Open: Tue–Sat lunch and dinner

Moderate

Excellent food at this friendly bistro, which isn't cheap but has a long-standing reliable reputation and an affordable wine list.

new arrivals in the 1940s, some of them escaping the terrors of Nazi Germany, only to be rounded up and sent to the concentration camps when the German armies finally invaded the French capital.

The Hôtel goes back to the 17th century, and takes its name from its original owner, the Duc de St-Aignan. The museum collection reaches back even further, and tells the story of Jewish history throughout France and Europe, also touching on other parts of the world. There are fascinating sections on such subjects as the effect of the French Revolution on the Jewish community and the Dreyfus Affair. This notable moment in French history occurred in 1894 when a Jewish army captain, Alfred Dreyfus, was accused and falsely convicted of spying for the Germans. To highlight the injustice, the very prominent author Émile Zola wrote an essay entitled *J'Accuse*, in which he turned the tables on the accusers and wrote passionately about the anti-Semitism in French society at the time. It made for very uncomfortable reading.

Some of the other features of the museum include works by artists such as Amedeo Modigliani who was of Jewish-Italian descent and Marc Chagall, born in

to an Hassidic family in Belorussia before establishing himself in Paris; elaborate robes and ancient scrolls and documents. *See also* the new and nearby Musée de la Shoah (Museum of the Holocaust), which opened recently (***see*** p.40).

Musée de la Chasse et de la Nature

Musée de la Chasse et de la Nature (8 mins)

Hôtel Guénégaud, 60 rue des Archives
***Tel**: (01) 53 01 92 40*
***Open**: Tue–Sun 11am–6pm*
***Adm**: adults €4.60, over-60s, students under-26 and 16–25s €2.30, under-5s free*

Yet another of the Marais mansions that is just as much worth seeing for the building itself as for what it contains – though in this case the Museum of Hunting and Nature is well worth the price of admission. The Hôtel, one of the finest mansions in the Marais, was designed in 1650 by the famous architect François Mansard for Henri de Guénégaud des Brosses, who was the French Secretary of State. It was remodelled in the 18th century and, more recently, was beautifully restored. For a time it was the home of the writer and politician, André Malraux, who opened the museum in 1967.

Today the house contains a collection devoted to nature, especially hunting, spread over three floors. It is surprisingly interesting, as specialist collections often are to anyone with a curious mind. There is the inevitable collection of stuffed animals, which usually produces mixed reactions in people, but some of them are genuine curios.

One section covers the weaponry of hunting, including primitive stone arrowheads and other prehistoric tools, through the development of knives and swords, then crossbows, guns and rifles. Some of them are real works of art, although you would not want to be on the wrong end of some of the larger crossbows, no matter how beautifully decorated with ivory and mother-of-pearl they might be.

There are a great number of fascinating paintings, many of them celebrating the beauty of nature and not merely its destruction. Included here are many works by Alexandre-François Desportes, regarded as one of France's finest wildlife artists, as well as work by Monet, Rembrandt and Rubens. There are also sculptures, ceramics, furniture, tapestries and other exquisite art objects, which are all well displayed.

BELLEVILLE

***See* Line 2, Ménilmontant, p.57**

Musée Edith Piaf p.57

Montmartre

LINE 12

PORTE DE LA CHAPELLE – MAIRIE D'ISSY

Work on Line 12 began in 1907 with the aim of linking the hilly village of Montmartre in northern Paris with Montparnasse in the south. It opened in 1910 and in the following years was extended at both ends. By 1930 the full 13.9km (8.7m) of line 12 had been built. From the visitor's point of view, the link between the two stations is still what matters, as it takes you by the splendid Musée d'Orsay. You can spend a morning in the museum (get there early to try to beat the crowds) and then hop on Line 12 to Abbesses and soak up the atmosphere of Montmartre in the afternoon and early evening.

LAMARCK CAULAINCOURT

Montmartre Vineyards 157

Musée de Montmartre

Avenue Junot 158

Moulin de la Galette 159

ABBESSES

Place des Abbesses 159

St-Jean l'Evangéliste de Montmartre 160

Espace Montmartre Salvador Dalì 161

Place du Tertre 162

St-Pierre de Montmartre 163

Sacré-Coeur, *see* Anvers p.54

PIGALLE

Place Pigalle, *see* p.54

ST-GEORGES

NOTRE-DAME-DE-LORETTE

TRINITÉ

ST-LAZARE

MADELEINE

Place de la Madeleine, *see* p.112

Eglise de la Madeleine, *see* p.113

Rue du Faubourg-St-Honoré, *see* p.114

CONCORDE

Place de la Concorde, *see* p.22

Jeu de Paume, *see* p.23

Musée de l'Orangerie, *see* p.24

ASSEMBLÉE NATIONALE

SOLFÉRINO

Musée d'Orsay 165

RUE DU BAC

Rue du Bac 167

SÈVRES-BABYLONE

RENNES

NOTRE-DAME-DES-CHAMPS

MONTPARNASSE-BIENVENUE

Tour Montparnasse, *see* p.76

Musée Antoine Bourdelle, *see* p.77

Jardin de l'Atlantique, *see* p.77

Musée de la Poste, *see* p.78

LAMARCK CAULAINCOURT

Au Lapin Agile (4 mins)

22 rue des Saules
***Tel**: (01) 46 06 85 87*
***Open**: Tue–Sun 9pm–2am*
***Adm**: €24*

Real Montmartre history is within the walls of this cabaret-cum-nightclub, where Renoir once waited on the tables and Picasso paid his drinks bill with one of his own paintings. The mind boggles to think of how much drink that painting could buy these days. Poets Verlaine and Apollinaire were also regulars, and the unusual name (the 'nimble rabbit') is a punning corruption of Lapin à Gill. The artist André Gill painted the club's first sign, which showed a rabbit leaping over the cooking pot. The cabaret continues, although you'll need a good knowledge of French to understand the jokes and songs.

Au Lapin Agile

Francis Labutte

122 rue Caulaincourt

Tel: (01) 42 23 58 26

Open: Mon–Sat 8.30am–2am, Sun 9am–2am, food served daily noon–4pm and 6.30–11pm

Inexpensive

Real neighbourhood café that caters to locals not tourists, and is all the better for it. Good plain food at good plain prices.

Au Pied du Sacré-Coeur

Square Caulaincourt

Tel: (01) 46 06 15 26

Open: Tue–Sun, lunch and dinner

Moderate

Despite the name, this is quite a way from Sacré-Coeur, but it's a lovely restaurant with an outdoor terrace, at the northern foot of the Montmartre hill. It's well away from the usual tourist haunts so you can expect the food here to be authentic, very French, and the place is always buzzing with locals.

Montmartre Vineyards (4 mins)

Rue des Saules

As unlikely as it may seem nowadays, Paris used to rival areas like Bordeaux and Burgundy as one of the country's leading wine-producing areas. Today only one small vineyard remains, and it isn't surprising to find it on the slopes of Montmartre, a part of Paris that has always been different. You can see the vines behind the Musée de Montmartre (***see** below*), although the vineyard can't be visited. If you wish to sample one of the 1,500 bottles produced each year, visit during the first weekend of October when the wine is auctioned for charity and everyone has a party. If you're lucky, you might be able to buy one in the shop at the Montmartre Museum.

Musée de Montmartre (5 mins)

12 rue Cortot
***Tel**: (01) 46 06 61 11;*
www.museedemontmartre.com
***Open**: Tue–Sun 10am–12.30pm and 1.30–6pm*
***Adm**: adults €4.50, over 60s and students €3.50, under-8s free*

The full name of this Montmartre mansion is Le Manoir de Rose de Rosimond, after the 17th-century actor belonging to Molière's company who once owned it. But it's a pity that the Montmartre Museum doesn't fulfil its promise, as a building devoted to the history of this area could be fascinating. This museum could be categorized as quite interesting rather than essential. The main attractions revolve around the house itself, rather than its fairly ordinary exhibits. The courtyard entrance is attractive, and gives a feel of the old days when Montmartre was a village. The views from the rear windows over the vineyards and the rooftops of northern Paris are also worth seeing.

The house could hardly have a better Montmartre pedigree as, at various times, it has been lived in by Dufy, Renoir, Utrillo and his artist mother, the lesser-known Suzanne Valadon. Exhibitions of paintings, prints and drawings explain Valadon's life a

Musée de Montmartre

little more, and tell of her relationship with her son. Some of the rooms have been decorated to try to give an impression of what life was like in Montmartre's late 19th-century heyday, including a recreated bistro and a zinc-topped bar.

Avenue Junot (3 mins)

Avenue Junot curls its way up from near the Métro through a part of Montmartre that's a little off the tourist track but full of interesting houses and history. Look for no.11, where a gate leads to the ***Hameau des Artistes***, a collection of studios where the modern day Montmartre artists live and work. The area is private but you can sneak a look if you can manage to be bold and discreet. At **no.13** several cartoon characters decorate the front of the house, as this used to be the home of the illustrator Francisque Poulbot, better-known to French people than to foreigners, while at no.15 is the **Maison Tristan Tzara**. The house was built in suitable style for the Romanian Dadaist poet, Tristan Tzara, and it certainly stands out from the crowd. From no.10 is a good view of the Moulin de la Galette (***see** opposite*).

Moulin de la Galette (4 mins)

79 rue Lepic

***Open**: not open to the public*

The high ground of Montmartre was once known for its windmills, including the notorious red windmill, the moulin rouge (***see*** p.51). The only genuine one remaining is here, on top of one of the area's hills, although it is sealed off from the public. If it looks familiar that's because it was once painted by Renoir, and other Montmartre artists have also featured it in their work. It marked the site of a famous dance hall, which was a very popular venue in the late 19th century, adding to the reputation of Montmartre as somewhere to go for drink, dance and a sample of the Bohemian lifestyle.

See also, Line 2, Blanche, p.51

Moulin Rouge p.51, Cimetière de Montmartre p.51, Musée de l'Érotisme p.52, Montmartre p. 53

Le Sancerre

35 rue des Abbesses

Tel: (01) 42 58 47 05

Open: daily, 7am–2am, food always available

Inexpensive

Simple food, cheap prices, buzzing atmosphere, pavement tables, non-touristy, a bit on the scruffy side – a real slice of modern Montmartre.

ABBESSES

Place des Abbesses (0 mins)

As you emerge from the Abbesses Métro, take a close look at the sign giving its name over the exit/entrance. It's probably the most photographed Métro sign in Paris, being a perfect surviving example of the original Art Nouveau décor that once adorned most of the underground network. The station is also of interest because it's the deepest one in Paris, as you'll know if you decided to ignore the elevator and walk up the steps instead. There are 285 of them, bringing you up some 91m (300ft) from the platform.

The Métro station, the square, the street and the area, all called Abbesses, take their name from the abbey that was here in the Middle Ages. In keeping with Montmartre's racy reputation, it's rumoured that the abbess at the abbey here had an affair in 1590 with Henri of Navarre, who went on to become Henri IV.

Abbesses Métro station

Despite the constant stream of visitors making their way up from here into the heart of Montmartre, the square and the streets around still maintain a very Parisian feel to them, as village-like as Montmartre itself (***see*** p.53), with cafés buzzing with local life, any of them worth a visit.

St-Jean l'Evangéliste de Montmartre (1 min)

19 rue des Abbesses
Tel*: (01) 46 06 43 96*
Open*: Mon–Sat 8.30am–noon and 3–7.30pm, Sun 3–6pm*
Adm*: free*

Designed by one Anatole de Baudot, and built between 1894 and 1904 (with a gap between 1898–1902), this church has the distinction of being the first in Paris to have been constructed using reinforced concrete – an innovative technique originally used to save money. It isn't exactly the prettiest of churches, having been built using a variety of styles and on completion, it soon acquired the nickname of 'St Jean of the Bricks', because of its red-brick frontage. In style, it is a curious mixture of Art Nouveau and Islamic design but is worth seeing for that reason alone. It also has a rather nice airy interior.

St-Jean l'Evangéliste de Montmartre

Au Virage Lepic

61 rue Lepic

Tel: (01) 42 52 46 79

Open: Wed–Mon, dinner only

Inexpensive

This is the kind of place every visitor to Montmartre hopes to find, but few do. It's worth the walk up from Abbesses to find it, along the street where Van Gogh used to live. It's the archetypal Parisian bistro with a zinc bar, Moulin Rouge posters on the walls, and excellent but inexpensive food, which is why it's recommended even though it only opens in the evening.

Éspace Montmartre Salvador Dalì (5 mins)

11 rue Poulbot

***Tel**: (01) 42 64 40 10*

***Open**: Sep–Jun daily 10am–6.30pm, Jul–Aug daily 10am–9pm*

***Adm**: adults €7, over-60s €6, students and 8–25s €5, under-8s free*

The artists most closely associated with Montmartre don't usually include the name of Salvador Dalì, but he had a studio in Montmartre and is as much a feature here as those other artistic geniuses who worked here, such as Picasso, Van Gogh and Renoir. Dalì arrived here in 1929 when he was 25 years old, and held his first Surrealist exhibition later that same year.

This cave-like and appropriately surreal museum is close to the location of Dalì's Montmartre studio, and has over 300 of the Catalan eccentric's works. This makes it the biggest collection of his material in France, although it is tiny in comparison with the Dalì Museum in Figueres, Spain.

The museum isn't to everyone's taste. The items do not include many of his best-known works, although the bright and bold sofa looking like a pair of red lips will be familiar to most visitors and some point out that much of the work on display

Espace Montmartre Salvador Dalì

comes from towards the end of the artist's life, when his faculties had deteriorated and he was repeating some of his successful themes, as well as churning out inferior work so that he could sign his name to it and bring in as much money as possible.

But, be that as it may, whether the best Dalì items are here or not, the gallery is well worth visiting by anyone remotely interested in the artist or in modern art generally. There are drawings, lithographs, sculptures, bronzes of melting clocks, paintings, and theatre and book designs, including an interesting collection of illustrations that Dalì made for *Alice in Wonderland*.

Some of the display areas have black walls, and there's a subterranean warren-like feel to the rooms. In some places Dalì's voice can be heard and, in others, there are hi-tech lighting and sound effects to dramatize the presentations. You can even buy some of the works, although if your budget won't stretch that far, the large gift shop offers a fun range of objects at lower prices. It's worth checking it out even if you don't want to see the museum, as it has some very unusual items.

Place du Tertre (6 mins)

Everyone who visits Montmartre or Sacré-Coeur seems to end up in the place du Tertre at some point, often all at the same time, it can seem sometimes from the crowds. It is probably the most touristy place in Paris, more noticeable than most because it is so small and because you don't need to look very far to see that the faces there are a real United Nations mix. The only locals you're likely to see are the artists who congregate in the square, making lightning sketches of the visitors, for whom no visit to Montmartre is complete without getting a portrait done. That said, the artists are mostly very talented and the prices reasonable.

However, there's more to the place du Tertre than speedy artists and restaurants

Place du Tertre

aimed squarely at the overseas visitors. The local artists have only been exhibiting their work here since the 19th century, when Montmartre's reputation as a haunt for Bohemian painters began.

The square can be traced back to the 14th century, and gets its name from the mound on which it stands, *tertre* meaning a mound or hillock in French. A scaffold stood here, used by the abbey as a not very Christian punishment for anyone who dared disobey its rules, which included a requirement for every local vineyard owner to hand over a quarter of his wine to the abbey. Quite a tax.

St-Pierre de Montmartre (6 mins)

2 rue du Mont-Cenis
***Tel**: (01) 46 06 57 63*
***Open**: daily 8.30am–7pm*
***Adm**: free*

With all eyes on Sacré-Coeur (***see*** p.54), the small neighbouring church of St Peter of Montmartre on the edge of the place du Tertre is usually overlooked. This is a great shame as it's of enormous historical interest. It mainly dates from the early 1130s, pre-dating Notre-Dame by 16 years, and is one of the contenders for being the oldest church in Paris – although when it was built it was a long way from the centre of the city. Note the variety of Early Gothic and Roman capitals on the columns.

St-Pierre de Montmartre

It is now all that remains of the original convent-abbey, which gave its name to the Abbesses area on the southern fringes of Montmartre (***see*** p.159). It was dedicated to St Peter in 1147 by Pope Eugene III, giving some idea of its importance at the time.

Some famous names are associated with the building, including the Italian poet Dante and later, St Ignatius Loyola, the founder of the Jesuits, who both visited and prayed here. Queen Adelaide, founder of the convent and wife of Louis VI, is buried here in the smallest cemetery in Paris, which contains just 85 graves. Among them are those of the sculptor Pigalle, who gives his name to place Pigalle further down the hill (***see*** p.54), and Louis Antoine de Bougainville, a French military officer, explorer and navigator, after whom the bougainvillea flower is named. You can also see a grave with a windmill on top, which marks the tomb of the Debray family, first owners of the Moulin de la Galette (***see*** p.159).

Sacre-Coeur, *see* Anvers, p.54

PIGALLE

***See* Line 2, Place Pigalle p.54**

MADELEINE

See Line 8, p.112

Place de la Madeleine p.112, Église de la Madeleine p.113
Rue du Faubourg-St-Honoré p.114

CONCORDE

See Line 1, p.22

Place de la Concorde p.22, Jeu de Paume p.23,
Musée de l'Orangerie p.24

SOLFÉRINO

Café des Hauteurs
Musée d'Orsay
Tel: (01) 45 49 42 33
Open: Tue–Sun, 10am–5pm
Inexpensive
Right by the Impressionist galleries, behind one of the old station's huge clocks, this café gives you views out over the river. The menu's simple but you can have anything from a cup of coffee to a proper meal, or just a sandwich or a bowl of soup – the food is highly recommended. It also has a faster turnaround than the restaurant.

Musée d'Orsay (4 mins)

1 rue de la Légion d'Honneur
***Tel**: (01) 40 49 48 14 and (01) 45 49 11 11 (recorded information) ; www.musee-orsay.fr*
***Open**: Jun–Sep Tue–Wed and Fri–Sat 9am–6pm, Thu 9am–9.45pm, Sun 9am–6pm; Oct–May Tue–Wed and Fri–Sat 10am–6pm, Thu 10am–9.45pm, Sun 9am–6pm*
***Adm**: adults €7 (€5 on Sun), 18–25s €5, under-18s free*

The Musée d'Orsay takes over where the Louvre (***see*** p.31) leaves off, concentrating on Western art from 1848 to 1914, when it hands over to the Modern Art Museum based in the Centre Georges Pompidou (***see*** p.148).

Of the three museums, the Orsay is probably the most popular. One reason is undoubtedly the building itself. The collection is housed in a former railway station that has been superbly converted to enhance its sense of light and space.

Built in 1900, to make it easier for people to get to the Paris Exposition that year, the station closed in 1939 and stood disused until the film director Orson Welles saw it as the ideal location for his 1962 version of Kafka's *The Trial*, after which it was used as an auction house and then as a theatre. Fortunately, plans in the 1970s to demolish it were abandoned in 1977, when it was decided that it should be converted into the stunning museum that exists today; it first opened its doors in 1986.

Inside, the building retains its open floor-

The original station clock at the Musée d'Orsay

to-ceiling expanse, with the upper galleries ranged along the walls. As the museum gets crowded, the best plan of attack is to get here early and take the lift straight to the upper level, not only because it's easier to walk down but because the upper level is where the most popular exhibits are – the superb collection of Impressionist and Post-Impressionist paintings. The paintings, by Van Gogh, of which there are several, including the world-famous *Bedroom at Arles*, are especially popular.

Other very familiar canvases – and it can be quite overpowering to see them for real – include Manet's *Le Déjeuner sur l'Herbe* and his *Olympia*, the naked courtesan, which was regarded as indecent when it was first shown in 1865. Monet's *Blue Waterlilies* are here, as are works by Degas, Toulouse-Lautrec, Gauguin and many more.

But the Impressionists are only a part of it. Here too are the Romantics, the Naturalists, the School of Pont-Aven, the Art Nouveau movement, and wonderful sculptures by the likes of Degas and Rodin. Degas also features in the photography collection, which numbers over 10,000 items, with space to display only a fraction of them.

The Musée d'Orsay Restaurant

Middle Level

Open: 11.45pm to 2.45pm, on Thu until 9.15pm

Inexpensive–moderate

If you stick to the cold buffet or take the main course and pud option, eating in here, in the original restaurant, with its turn-of-the-century décor, of the hotel of the Gare d'Orsay need not be expensive. Get here early as it tends to fill up quickly. A kids' menu is also available.

Rue du Bac

La Frégate

1 rue du Bac

Tel: (01) 42 61 23 77

Open: daily 7am–midnight, food available 11.30am–11.30pm

Moderate

This upmarket café at the river end of the rue du Bac has a view over the Seine. It serves food most of the day and has a terrace, bar and restaurant.

RUE DU BAC

Rue du Bac (1 min)

This characterful old street dates all the way back to 1564 and was named after the ferry (*bac*) that used to sail to and fro across the Seine from the end of the street, where the Pont Royal now is, taking stone across the river when the Tuileries Palace was being built that year. Later there was a barracks here, where the three musketeers from Dumas' famous novel were based – though fiction, the characters were all real. Whether the apparition of the Virgin Mary, said to have been seen in 1830 by a nun at the convent that existed here then, was real or imaginary, who knows?

MONTPARNASSE - BIENVENUE

See Line 4, p.76

Tour Montparnasse p.76, Musée Antoine Bourdelle p.77, Jardin de l'Atlantique p.77, Musée de la Poste p.78

La Défense

FURTHER AFIELD

This book covers the central zone of Paris and if you are only here for a few days or it's your first visit, there is more than enough to entertain and interest you. However, 10-30 minutes beyond the centre, there are several sights accessible by Métro or by the RER, which also runs through the centre of Paris. If you want one day out, the obvious choice is Versailles (*see* p.179); for kids and the young at heart, Disneyland Paris will be appealing, although a single day will be long and possibly frustrating. If using the RER, take note that French trains are usually punctual so leave plenty of time.

Château de Vincennes

Bois de Vincennes (4 mins)

***Open**: daily, dawn–dusk*
***Adm**: free*

While Baron Haussmann was occupying himself with the Bois de Boulogne to the west of Paris (***see** p.171*), his landscape architect Adolphe Alphand was busy working on the Bois de Vincennes in the southeast. The woods had always been here and had been a royal hunting ground since the 11th century. It was only in 1860 that Napoleon III gave them to the city of Paris so that Haussmann's team could transform them into the kind of public park that had become popular in England.

The park at Vincennes is nowhere near as large as the Bois de Boulogne (***see** p.171*) but it still provides a pleasant day out. There's boating on the lake, a big amusement park, a zoo, various flower gardens and a château.

Château de Vincennes (10 mins)

Avenue de Paris, www.monum.fr
***Tel**: (01) 48 08 31 20*
***Open**: Summer May 2–Aug 30, 10am–12pm and 1pm–6pm (1st guided tour at 10:15, last guided tour at 5:15); Winter: Sep 1 – Apr 30: closes 5pm (1st guided tour at 10:15, last guided tour at 4:15;*
***Adm**: adults €6.10, concessions €4.10 (75-min tour), €4.60/€3.10 (45-min tour), under-18s free*

This impressive château dates back to the 14th century. It was originally a hunting lodge but then became a royal palace (the English king Henry V died here in 1422) until the Court moved out to Versailles in 1682 (***see** p.179*). It is the only fortified castle near Paris, has also been used as a prison and Napoleon used it as an arsenal. Since then it had slowly crumbled and suffered bomb-damaged in World War II. It has recently been successfully renovated and you can now visit two small museums, the royal chapel, fortified enclosure and the moat. The dungeons are currently closed.

Porte Maillot

Bois de Boulogne (2 mins)

***Open**: open access*
Also accessible from Métro Les Sablons

Despite this park on the western edge of the city being 865 ha (2135 acres) in size, it can still get crowded, especially on summer weekends when it sometimes seems that half of Paris is here enjoying its facilities. These include museums, cycling, boating, a bowling alley, a theatre, a sports stadium, a château (given to the park's designer, Baron Haussmann by Napoleon III – closed to the public), riding, lakes, restaurants and even two race-courses (***see** p.176*).

There are two lakes with boats for hire and a motor boat to take you to and from the islands for a walk or a memorable meal at one of the restaurants (***see** below*). The lakes are *Lac Inférieur*, which is confusingly the larger of the two, and the smaller one is called *Lac Supérieur*.

Also within the park there are other smaller parks, such as the *Parc de Bagatelle*; within the Parc de Bagatelle there are even smaller specialist areas, including a lovely rose garden (at its peak in June) and different styles of garden such as English or Japanese. The *Pré Catelan Park* is in the very centre of the Bois de Boulogne and here you'll find lawns and woods, and a 200-year-old beech tree whose spread of branches is said to be the largest of any tree in Paris. Elsewhere, the 19th-century *Jardin des Serres d'Auteuil* has a palm house with tropical plants, surrounded by greenhouses growing ornamental hothouse plants. The *Shakespeare Garden* is a novelty garden, that contains every tree, flower, plant and herb mentioned in Shakespeare's plays, and close by is an *open-air theatre*. No prizes for guessing which plays are popular.

N.B: Although the park is fine during the day, it is best avoided after dark, when parts of it attract some rather disreputable characters.

Jardin d'Acclimatation (15 mins)

Boulevard des Sablons, Bois de Boulogne
***Tel**: (01) 40 67 90 82;*
www.jardinacclimatation.fr
***Open**: daily, 10am–7pm (closes 6pm Oct–May)*
***Adm**: adults and children over 2 €2.50, under-3s free*

The Jardin d'Acclimatation has a zoo, which includes a farm and a pets' corner, an amusement park and a Herb Museum designed specially for children.

Musée National des Arts et Traditions Populaire (20 mins)

6 avenue du Mahatma-Gandhi, Bois de Boulogne
***Tel**: (01) 44 17 60 00*
***Open**: Wed–Sun 9.30am–5pm*
***Adm**: adults €4, students, 10–25s, over-60s €2.60, under-10s free, and free admission on first Sun of each month*

The 'adult' museum is the Musée National des Arts et Traditions Populaire. Despite being a national museum it's quite small, and provides a very interesting insight into the ordinary lives of people in rural and city areas before the Industrial Revolution.

Hippodrome d'Auteuil,
see Line 10, Porte d'Auteuil, p.176

Hippodrome de Longchamp,
see Line 10, Porte d'Auteuil, p.176

Parc des Princes sports stadium,
see Line 9, Porte de St-Cloud, p.176

Grande Arche de la Défense

La Défense (1 min)

***Tel**: (01) 49 07 27 57; www.grandearche.com*
***Open**: daily, 10am–7pm*
***Adm**: adults €7.50, students, 6–18s €6, under-6s free*

One of the reasons Paris is such an attractive city is that the centre isn't marred by high-rise buildings. With a few notable exceptions, such as the Eiffel Tower and the Tour Montparnasse, the city skyline is mainly made up of buildings no more than a few storeys high, many

Les Communautes

Hilton Hotel, La Défense

Tel: (01) 46 92 10 10; www.hilton.com

Open: Mon–Fri lunch, Mon–Thu dinner, Sat–Sun 7am–11am

Expensive

Fine dining in the Hilton Hotel, worth it for the splendid view over the Grande Arche itself, although there are plenty of cheaper options nearby as well.

of them still the beautiful old offices and apartment buildings with their lovely rooftops.

So where do the ever-increasing offices go, that every city needs? Paris's answer was to develop La Défense as a business and government district, but to do it in style and make an attraction out of it in its own right. They used cutting-edge architectural design, outdoor sculptures, trendy shopping centres – lots of steel, glass, reflections and sharp angles. On a sunny day with clear blue skies the effect is dazzling.

The most dazzling feature of all, no matter what the weather, is the *Grande Arche*. This illustrates perfectly the flair and thought that went into the design of the whole complex. It is a simple yet futuristic open block, exactly in line with the Champs Élysées (***see*** p.19), the Arc de Triomphe, which is 6km (3.75 miles) away (***see*** p.14) and, beyond that, with the Arc du Carrousel (***see*** p.29) outside the Louvre. This links it with the past while looking to the future, and shows the continuity of the city. From a distance it looks as if the walls are solid blocks, that it is a giant monument echoing the shape of the Arc de Triomphe. But as you get closer you see that the sides are functional, too and contain offices.

The Grande Arche stands 110m (360ft) high, so high that Notre-Dame cathedral could fit beneath it and wider than the Champs-Élysées. From the top (and the high-speed ride up there in the glass lift is quite something) you can see that the Eiffel Tower and, beyond it, the Tour Montparnasse also line up. There is a restaurant up there but you don't get a good view. Better to eat elsewhere and enjoy a view of the Arche and La Défense itself.

A Danish architect, Johan Otto von Spreckelsen, designed the Arche, and it was opened in 1989 for the Bicentenary of the French Revolution. Sadly, he died before the work was completed so he never saw his own creation. The name La Défense, incidentally, comes from the Franco–

Prussian War and a brave stand by French soldiers against the Prussians in 1870.

The Arche straddles a pedestrian square known as *Le Parvis*, which on weekdays is filled with the people who work in the area. All around the square are fountains and sculptures, including work by Miró. You can get a guide to La Défense from the information kiosk ('Info-Défense'), which is in front of the CNIT Exhibition Hall.

LINE 4

Porte de Clignancourt

Marché aux Puces de St-Ouen (4 mins)

17 avenue de la Porte de Clignancourt
***Open**: Sat–Mon 7am–6pm*

There are several flea (*puce*) markets in Paris, but the one at St-Ouen, near the northern end of Line 4, is the biggest and the oldest in the city. It goes back to the 19th century when the 'Porte' of Clignancourt was actually a gateway into the city, outside which people would gather, hoping to sell some of their clothes and other items to the Parisians leaving and re-entering the city. Today there are 2,000 official stalls and many more unofficial stalls and stretches of pavement in the streets around that attract thousands of people every day, and tens of thousands at weekends. You can buy furniture, clothes, household goods, antiques, paintings, jewellery and just plain junk.

Le Soleil

109 avenue Michelet, St-Ouen

Tel: (01) 40 10 08 08

Open: daily lunch and Thu–Sat dinner

Expensive

Worth going to the flea market just to eat in this fashionable bistro. Not cheap, but worth it.

LINE 7

Porte de la Villette

Parc de la Villette (2 mins)

Avenue Corentin-Cariou, www.villette.com
***Tel**: (01) 40 03 75 75*
***Open**: daily; restricted access 1am–6pm*

In keeping with the city's belief in developing its sometimes run-down further reaches, northeast Paris has been made home to this collection of mainly science-based museums, spread across 55 hectares (136 acres) of parkland, where the city slaughterhouses and livestock market used to be. It's easy to reach from Line 7 and there's enough to occupy a whole day, especially for families. Check out the Villette card (€15 for one person, €24 for two), which will give you discounts on entries to tours, some events and sights within the park.

Cité de la Musique

221, avenue Jean Jaurès
www.cite-musique.fr
***Tel**: (01) 44 84 45 45.*
***Open**: Museum Tue–Sat 12pm–6pm, Sun 10am –6pm.*

On either side of the entrance is the *Cité de la Musique*, though the main interest here for daytime visitors is the excellent, modern museum. Headphones (English commentary available) give you the sound of instruments as you approach them and there are live musicians, computer displays and models of theatres and concert halls. Guided tours are also available.

Cité des Sciences

30, avenue Corentin-Cariou,
www.cite-sciences.fr
***Tel:** (08) 92 69 70 72 from abroad (0)1 46 91 57 56 (Mon–Sat 9am–7pm) or book on line at www.fnac.com*
***Open**: Tues–Sat; 10am–6pm; Sun, closes 7pm*
www.cite-sciences.fr

At the far end of the park is the *Cité des Sciences*, which is a vast and futuristic science museum, with planetarium, temporary exhibitions, interactive videos, computer-controlled robots and models of space rockets and space stations that you can explore.

Géode

***Tel:** (01) 40 05 79 99*
www.villette.com
***Open**: Tue–Sun 10.30am– 9.30pm, 7.30pm on Sun*
***Adm**: adult €8.75, concessions € 6.75; every evening after 6.30pm admission to two films for €11.*

Near the Science Museum is the Géode, an IMAX cinema with a screen of 1000 sq m (11,000 sq ft). On one side of the Géode is a high-tech yet simple kids' playground, but if the dragon slide seems too tame, take them into the nearby *Cineaxe*, another IMAX-style cinema, with a huge screen and moving seats so that bobsleigh rides and motorbike races are all too real.

LINE 9

Porte de Saint-Cloud

Parc des Princes sports stadium

24, rue du Commandant Guilbaud, Bois de Boulogne
***Tel**: (01) 42 30 03 60*

On the edge of the Bois de Boulogne, this stadium was built for the 1998 Soccer World Cup and was the proposed main stadium for Paris's 2012 Olympic bid. It hosts many rugby and football matches and is also the home of the *National Sports Museum*.

LINE 10

Porte d'Auteuil

Hippodrome d'Auteuil

Route des Lacs, Bois de Boulogne
***Tel**: (01) 40 71 47 47*

One of the two horse tracks in the Bois de Boulogne (***see*** p.171), this is where steeplechases are run.

Hippodrome de Longchamp

Route des Tribunes Bois de Boulogne
www.france-galop.com
***Tel**: (01) 44 30 75 00)*
***Open** for racing: 25 Mar–24 Oct*

Also in the Bois de Boulogne (***see*** p.171), this is home to the famous Prix de l'Arc de Triomphe race held on the first weekend in October. There's free child care (0–10 years), free pony rides and nappy-changing facilities if you have a young family in tow.

Marne-la-Vallée/Chessy

Disneyland®Resort Paris (2 mins)

Marne-la-Vallée
Tel: *(01) 60 30 60 30, www.disneylandparis.com*
Open: *Jul–Aug daily 9am–11pm, Apr–Jun daily 9am–8pm, Sep–Mar Mon–Fri 10am–6pm Sat–Sun 9am–8pm*
Adm: *one-day pass: adults €39, 3–11s €29, under-3s free*

Disneyland® Resort Paris is just 40 minutes by train from central Paris with the RER station right outside the entrance. If you are just there for the day, aim to arrive as early as possible, stay as late as possible, and be prepared for the fact that you might want to spend more than one day there. There's a lot to see and some rides that children (and even adults) will want to go on more than once. If you want to stay, there are seven hotels and a golf course.

There are three distinct areas to Disneyland® Resort Paris: *Disneyland*, the *Walt Disney Studios Park* and *Disneyland Village*. You do want to believe everything you see in Disneyland – young children certainly will and even adults will find themselves bowled along by it all, and marvelling at the sheer brilliance of the technical effects on some of the rides. Some of it might be corny, but it's classy corn.

As with the parks in America, there are five different 'lands': *Fantasyland®*, *Discoveryland®*, *Frontierland®*, *Adventureland®* and *Main Street USA®*. This last looks back to the old-fashioned American Main Street, with parades, shops and Disney characters wandering around. *Frontierland®* re-creates the magic of the wild west, but with a little bit of poetic licence so that it incorporates the very clever *Phantom Manor* as well as the thrills of the runaway train ride.

If younger children find Phantom Manor a bit frightening – and the holographic ghosts are very convincing – *Fantasyland®*, might be the answer with its tot-friendly rides such as the *Mad Hatter's Tea Cups*,

Dumbo the Flying Elephant and the ever-popular *It's A Small World*. This is the ultimate Disney experience, which might have adults screaming at the cuteness of it, but youngsters usually adore it.

Finally there's *Discoveryland*®, with the *Space Mountain* ride whizzing you round in the pitch black, and *Adventureland*® with two of the most popular rides in the park: *Pirates of the Caribbean* and *Indiana Jones and the Temple of Doom*. And if you can do all that in one day, you're doing well.

The *Walt Disney Studios Park*® is the other side of the coin from Disneyland. Where Disneyland is all about fantasy, the Studios Park is about the reality (and the illusion) of movie-making. Anyone who has visited Universal Studios in Los Angeles or the Disney-MGM Studios in Florida will know what to expect. There's the *Production Courtyard* where you can have a scary ride through *Catastrophe Canyon* or the *Stunt Show Spectacular*, which shows just what can be done with cars and motorbikes in those thrilling car chase scenes. There are other areas and other displays that cover animation techniques and the tricks of the trade, showing why you shouldn't believe everything you see on the cinema screen.

You will probably spend least time in the *Disney Village*®, which is where all the bars, cafés, shops, restaurants, nightclubs, cinemas and theatres are. You are only likely to spend time here if you are staying at the resort.

Fontainebleau-Avon

Château de Fontainbleau

(15 mins – shuttle bus)

Tel: *(01) 60 71 50 70 (booking ahead is advisable), www.musee-chateau-fontainebleau.fr*

Open: *Château: Wed–Mon Oct-May 9.30am–5pm; Jun–Sep 9.30pm–6pm Gardens: daily 9am–5pm Nov-Feb; Mar–Apr and Oct 9am–7pm (English garden shuts an hour before other gardens)*

Adm: *Grands Appartements: adults €5.50, concessions €4, under-18s free and on first Sun*

of the month; €3 extra for use of audioguides
Petits Appartements: tours only, adults €3, concessions €2.3, under-14s free and on the first Sun of the month
You can buy a ticket at the SNCF counter for all travel and museum entry.

A 35-minute trip from the Gare de Lyon (Line 1), this is a lovely day out. Like Versailles (***see** below*) and the Château de Vincennes (***see*** p.170), the palace at Fontainebleau was originally a hunting lodge, standing in a vast forest. This all changed in the early 16th century when François I (a contemporary of England's Henry VIII) turned it into a renaissance palace – one of the finest royal palaces in the whole of France.

Its architecture and decoration spans from the 12th to the 19th century (one 12th-century tower still remains) and it was a favourite palace of all France's sovereigns, including Napoleon who received the Pope here when he crowned him in 1804. The beautiful double staircase at the front is mid-17th-century and was designed by Androuet du Cerceau and the renaissance decoration is the work of both Italian and Flemish craftsmen, whose work gave rise to the term, 'School of Fontainebleau'. The palace is now a UNESCO world heritage sight.

RER C5

Versailles-Rive Gauche

Château de Versailles (7 mins)

***Tel**: (01) 30 83 76 20; www.chateauversailles.fr*
***Open**: Apr–Oct Tue–Sun 9am–6pm, Mar Tue–Sun 9am–5pm*
***Adm**: adults €7.50 (€5.30 after 3.30pm), under-18s free*
You can buy a ticket at the SNCF counter for all travel and museum entry.

It is very easy to get to Versailles – just 40 minutes on the RER, which you can catch at Invalides (Line 13), Champ de Mars Tour Eiffel (Line 6) or St-Michel Notre-Dame stations (walk there from St Michel, Line 4 or Cluny la Sorbone, Line 10).

The former royal palace of Versailles is one of the biggest and grandest châteaux in France, so sumptuous and huge that it takes your breath away. Compared with the conditions of the poor, it's clear why the French Revolution took place. The palace owes its existence to the fact that Louis XIV, the Sun King, was jealous of the château at Vaux-le-Vicomte, which was owned by his finance minister. Louis determined to build himself a château that would put this one in the shade… and he succeeded. He hired the team that had been responsible for Vaux-le-Vicomte and told them to build him something a hundred times bigger. They came up with the biggest palace in Europe, with room for (and a need for) up to 20,000 people to cope with the upkeep.

When work began in 1668, there was only a small hunting lodge on the vast Versailles estate. By 1682 the château was so appealing that Louis XIV moved his court here from the centre of Paris. In 1789, when Louis XVI was on the throne and the rumblings of the Revolution could be heard, the king and his queen were forced to move out of Versailles and back to Paris, to try to deal with the simmering unrest. Four years later they were both dead, and by 1833 Versailles had become a state museum.

It's a short walk from the station to the château, the road leading up through the original entrance gate, designed by Mansart, taking you into the vast courtyard. There are buildings ahead, and to left and right, dwarfing the visitors. And what you cannot yet see are the grounds beyond, which in their turn dwarf the buildings. The ticket offices are straight ahead, past the statue of Louis XIV, through the *Royal Courtyard*, which only the royal carriages were permitted to enter, and beyond that the *Marble Courtyard*,

Marée de Versailles

22 rue au Pain, Versailles

Tel: (01) 30 21 73 73

Open: Tue–Sat lunch and dinner

Expensive

Fresh fish is a speciality here, and a beautiful terrace to dine on, in keeping with the opulence of the palace at Versailles.

surrounded by the main palace buildings.

Either side of the Royal Courtyard are the *North* and *South Wings*, the North Wing containing such breathtaking sights as the *Royal Chapel* and the palace's private opera house. In the main buildings that surround the Marble Courtyard and Royal Courtyard are rooms that include the *King's Bedroom* (where Louis XIV died at the age of 77), the *Queen's Bedroom* and probably the most astonishing room of all, the *Hall of Mirrors*. This runs for 70m (233ft), almost the full length of the back of the house, and is filled with mirrors, windows and glistening chandeliers. Although it is currently under restoration, you can still see parts of it.

There are just as many wonderful things to see in the gardens behind the palace, which is why you should allow as full a day as possible for a visit. The several pools and fountains are magical, and the geometric gardens lead down to the *Grand Canal*; off to one side is the *Petit Trianon*, the miniature château that became a favourite retreat for Marie-Antoinette.

From a practical point of view, there are different entrances to the palace depending on what you want to see. All are clearly marked. One allows access to the Hall of Mirrors, the State Apartments and other rooms, for a self-guided visit. Another leads to the King's Bedroom, for which you will be given an audioguide. A third entrance is where the guided tours start, and it is worth considering one of these first as they include the main rooms plus others that you cannot visit any other way. You should arrive early to find out the times of particular tours in particular languages and to reserve a place, or phone ahead. Don't worry that if you arrive too soon you may find yourself killing time till a tour starts – you can easily spend a few hours exploring the grounds and return for a booked tour later.

PRACTICAL INFORMATION

Finding somewhere to stay

There are lots of options in Paris for finding a hotel. These are some useful resources.

Office de Tourisme et des Congrès de Paris

www.paristouristoffice.com
Tel: *(08) 92 68 30 30 (recorded info in English and French at €0.34 per minute)*

The Tourist Board runs a service dealing with hotel accommodation. ***See*** *also* below.

La Centrale de Réservations (FUAJ-HI)

4, boulevard, Jules Ferry, www.fuaj.fr
Tel: *(01) 43 57 02 60*
Métro: *République*
Open: *daily 8am–10pm*
Provides same-day reservations in one of their affiliated youth hostels.

Late Booking

Booking through the internet on a last-minute deal can give you some very good discounts. Even if you book ahead, some hotels offer discounts for web bookings.
www.laterooms.com
www.lastminute.com
www.expedia.co.uk
www.paris.org.hotels/OR/
www.france-hotel-guide.com/parishotels.htm
www.parischarminghotels.net
www.bootiquehotels.com
www.hoteldirect.co.uk
www.perfectlyparis.com
www.parisbandb.com
www.travelwithkids.about.com/od/paris/a/

Tourist Information

Office de Tourisme et des Congrès de Paris

25–27 rue des Pyramides
Tel: *(**see** above);* ***Open***: *Mon–Sat 9am–6.30pm*
Métro: *Tuileries*

The office offers a vast amount of information and the staff speak several languages.

Ile-de-France Tourist Information

Carrousel du Louvre, 99 rue de Rivoli
www.pidf.com

***Tel**: (01) 4450 1998; **Open**: daily*
***Métro**: Palais Royal, Musee du Louvre*

There is another office at the entrance to Disneyland® Resort Paris (***see** p.177*).

Entertainment

The best sources of information for what's on in Paris, from clubs to restaurants, cinemas, concerts and theatre, are Paris's weekly entertainment magazines, *Pariscope* (which has an English-language section), *L'Officiel des Spectacles* and *Zurban*. Of the daily newspapers, *Le Figaro* and *Le Parisien* both have a section on Paris and *The Herald Tribune* published in Paris in English can also be useful.

Smart restaurants will need to be booked in advance, especially in the evenings. Many restaurants offer a *Formule* or fixed-price menu, often for three courses. The quality varies although prices can be low.

For nightlife, the most happening spots are near Menilmontant (Line 2) and Parmentier (Line 3), the Bastille (Lines, 1, 5, 8), and the Marais (Line 1). The Champs-Élysées (Lines 1 and 13), is beginning to flourish again with stylish singles bars on the roads leading off it, although it's still pretty much tourists frequenting the main boulevard. Partying goes on late into the night (or morning) at weekends but tends to shut down around 2am during the week.

Tickets for large-scale concerts and events can be booked at **FNAC** book/music shops or online at *www.fnac.com*. Cheaper, same-day tickets are available through **Kiosques Théâtre** (***see** below*). Half-price tickets are also available at several private theatres during the first week of each new show. Check the weekly guides for details.

Kiosques Théâtre

Across from 15 place de la Madeleine,
***Métro**: Madeleine*
15 place Raoul Dautry
***Métro**: Montparnasse Bienvenue*
***Open**: Tue–Sat 12.30pm-8pm and Sun 12.30pm–4pm*

Paris Museum Card

This is good value and lets you into over 70 museums. For more information, ***see*** *www.museums-of-paris.com*

1-day pass	€25
3-day pass (consecutive days)	€44
5-day pass (consecutive days)	€62

Paris City Passport

www.en.parisinfo.com/

Price:€5

This entitles you to discounts for sights and attractions chosen by the Paris Convention and Visitors Bureau. You need to buy it on line in advance.

Opening Hours

Shops are usually open Mon–Sat 9.30am–6.30pm. Some smaller shops break for lunch (often 1pm–3pm). There is limited Sunday opening. Late night shopping is Wednesday or Thursday until about 8pm.

Traditional restaurant hours are usually 12pm–3pm and 7.30pm–9.30pm, although some restaurants keep their kitchens open later. A service charge of 15% is usually included in the bill. Most people leave the waiter the small change if paying in cash.

Emergency Numbers

Paramedics (SAMU) ***Tel***: 15
Police ***Tel***: 17
Fire department (*Pompiers*) ***Tel***: 18
Ambulance (SAMU) ***Tel***: 15
Emergency (from a mobile phone) ***Tel***: 112
Doctor (*SOS Médecin*) ***Tel***: (01) 43 37 77 77
Dentist (*SOS Dentaire*) ***Tel***: (01) 43 37 51 00
English Language Crisis Line (SOS Help)
Tel: (01) 43 23 80 80; ***Open***: 3pm–11pm daily

Useful numbers

Operator *Tel*: 12
Directory Enquiries *Tel*: 12
International Operator *Tel*: 00 33 12 then country code
International Directory Enquiries *Tel*: 00 32 12 then country code (costs €3 per call)

INDEX

D

E

F

G

H

M

R

Acknowledgements

The publishers would like to thank Antonia Cunningham for her invaluable help in bringing the book together, Mike Gerrard, and Irena Stupar for the photography.

Photo credits